Enjoy!

Claire & Kevin
1409 Waters Edge Dr.
Roswell, GA 30075

Know you'll enjoy
this little book. :)

FY25CSCSLNP

Reedy Press
PO Box 5131
St. Louis, MO 63139, USA
www.reedypress.com

Library of Congress Control Number: 2024930276

ISBN: 9781681065298

Design by Jill Halpin

Cover photo credits, clockwise from top: Desposito's Seafood, courtesy of Desposito's Seafood; Brandon Carter of Common Thread, courtesy of Cameron Wilder; fried chicken from Mrs. Wilkes' Dining Room, courtesy of Rebekah Faulk Lingenfelser; Strange Bird, courtesy of SV Images; Praline Basket dessert at The Olde Pink House Restaurant & Tavern, courtesy of The Olde Pink House Restaurant & Tavern.

Back cover photo credits: see credits for these photos on their interior pages.

Back cover headshot courtesy of Sarah Peacock.

Photos by author unless otherwise noted.

Title page photo credits, starting from top row left to right: HUSK, photo by Andrew Lee; Cotton & Rye; Leopold's Ice Cream; Cohen's Retreat; Tequila's Town Mexican Restaurant; Paula Deen's The Lady & Sons, photo by Kelli Boyd Photography; B. Matthew's Eatery, photo by Blake Studwell; Auspicious Baking Co.; Erica Davis Lowcountry; Common Thread, photo by SV Images; Collins Quarter; Lulu's Chocolate Bar.

Printed in the United States of America
24 25 26 27 28 5 4 3 2 1

UNIQUE EATS AND EATERIES

OF

THE PEOPLE AND STORIES BEHIND THE FOOD

REBEKAH FAULK LINGENFELSER

Seafood Tower at HUSK.
Photo courtesy of
Andrew Cebulka

DEDICATION

For my handsome and hard-working husband,
Kurt Hopkins Lingenfelser, a twelfth-generation Savannahian,
lover of good food, and the shrimp to my grits.

The Bamboo Room Tiki Bar at Sorry Charlie's
Photo courtesy of Sorry Charlie's

CONTENTS

ACKNOWLEDGMENTS

I met so many amazing people while writing this book. There are several to thank, and I'll start with the restaurant owners, managers, and chefs who demonstrated genuine hospitality by taking the time to sit down with me and share their stories. Your restaurants and recipes make this city uniquely special, and it was an honor to get to know you all better.

Thank you to the marketing professionals who provided beautiful photographs and confirmed facts. Your timely responses and contributions were truly helpful. To my friend and former colleague Joshua Peacock, thank you for reviewing my early pages and sharing thoughtful feedback in the midst of welcoming your new baby girl into the world.

Special thanks to my friend and neighbor, Rebecca Phillips, aka Becki, a fellow writer and fierce editor. You volunteered your time, finding all my run-on sentences, pointing out my favorite recurring words, and offering excellent suggestions, ultimately making this a better book. I appreciate you more than you know!

I'd also like to thank my family and friends for pushing me forward and spurring me onward when the project felt overwhelming. To my husband, Kurt, thank you for believing in me and for reaffirming me when I needed encouragement most. You will always be my favorite dining partner.

I am grateful to the Reedy Press team for inviting me to take on this project. I was ecstatic when I received your email, and the timing and fit could not have been more perfect. While writing this book, I was also finishing culinary school. The two projects together brought me so much happiness.

Dear reader, thank you too, for picking up this book. I hope you'll devour it, page by page, just as you will many delicious plates during your time in alluring Savannah, Georgia.

INTRODUCTION

Recently, *Travel + Leisure* described Savannah's food scene as one of the American South's most exciting food destinations, noting how over a short span of time the Hostess City of the South has become a "full-fledged foodie mecca." I arrived in Savannah in December of 2016, just in time to witness this growth and transformation. With million-dollar expansions on the east and west ends of River Street, a new food truck park, elevated fine-dining restaurants in the most gorgeous Victorian mansions, and an influx of ethnic cafés offering a breadth of international cuisines, Savannah's dining scene has become competitive with some of the nation's top food destinations. It can be as upscale or as laid back as you choose.

I wish I had a nickel for every time the names "Johnny Harris Restaurant" or "William's Seafood" came up in conversation during my interviews with locals and restaurateurs for this book. Though both are closed now, they were Savannah institutions in their day, well-respected restaurants still fondly considered by many who cherish countless good memories there. During the writing of this book, our seaside city suffered the loss of two delicious Southern, coastal restaurants, both of which were rare jewels and waterfront gems: Pearl's Saltwater Grille Seafood and Steaks and Paula Deen's Creek House Seafood & Grill. Sadly, Pearl's was destroyed by fire in August of 2022, and Paula Deen's Creek House closed its doors just a few months later. Conversely, Desposito's Seafood, a beloved seafood shack on the riverbanks in Thunderbolt, celebrated the most anticipated restaurant reopening in Savannah recently, after closing in 2020.

The restaurant industry is known to have one of the highest business failure rates in the country. Eateries come and go, opening and closing sometimes before you realize they were ever there. In choosing which ones to include for this book, those that have stood the test of time made the top of my list, while others stood out for being founded in Savannah or for offering a menu item or dining experience you can't find anywhere else. These are not franchises (although some hope to become franchised) or chain restaurants, but in most cases are locally owned small businesses started by hardworking people fulfilling their American dream. Representing Savannah well geographically was also important. While there are many delectable destinations on River Street and downtown, the city has quite a few worthy locales in outlying areas that should not be overlooked. A blend of in-depth research and personal dining experiences helped to determine the final outcome.

Unique Eats and Eateries of Savannah showcases the people and stories behind the food. Meeting those people and hearing their stories helped me understand the city better, and as a result I have an even deeper appreciation for it. As you read this book, I'm certain you will, too.

So, my friends, the 84 restaurants contained in this book showcase some of the best of Savannah's one-of-a-kind food establishments. I hope you'll visit each one, discover something new, and enjoy every bite of the journey. Bon appétit, y'all!

Author Rebekah Faulk Lingenfelser and Marcia Thompson, granddaughter of Mrs. Sema Wilkes.

Erica Davis Lowcountry's shrimp and grits
Photo courtesy of Erica Davis Lowcountry

UNIQUE EATS AND EATERIES

OF

THE BURGER BOAT

Hooked on freshness, overboard on taste

Steve Martin has two passions: cooking and being on the water. A chef and native Floridian, he and his wife, Margo, have found a way to marry those passions in one of Savannah and the South Carolina Lowcountry's most unique food stands on the water—The Burger Boat. Brightly colored and easy to spot, this floating hamburger stand is easy to find on any given day anchored in one of coastal Georgia's many popular waterways or docked at a busy marina or sandbar.

Satisfying hungry boaters and island hoppers everywhere, the local menu features handcrafted, 100 percent grass-fed beef burgers, all-natural patty melts, and even veggie burgers, all served with chips and a pickle. Chef Steve says the cheeseburger is the most popular menu item, but burgers aren't the only thing he's cooking up. With 30 years' experience as a chef, he knows the key to keeping his customers coming back is serving good-quality food. Everything is prepped day-of on the boat. You can also enjoy Wiley's Championship BBQ pulled pork, all-beef 100 percent kosher seven-inch hot dogs, Jamaican jerk chicken, and your choice of tacos—fish, shrimp or grilled chicken—the second most popular dish.

After searching Facebook Marketplace, the Martins found a used pontoon boat for sale in upstate New York and had it shipped to Savannah on a semitruck. It would require a few renovations, like redesigning the kitchen, installing a new 115-horsepower Yamaha

The Burger Boat is eco-friendly, using no plastic or styrofoam, and serving food in biodegradable takeout containers that, if dropped in the water, disintegrate within a matter of days.

Left: You can't miss The Burger Boat's tie-dye colors cruising along the waterways. *Right:* The juicy, double Swiss grass-fed hamburger all the way, served with chips and a pickle. All photos courtesy of The Burger Boat.

motor, and meeting health department codes. Once they fought their way through the red tape, they got the boat in the water only to find the 22-inch aluminum pontoons were not enough to keep it afloat. With some adjustments, including filling the pontoons with foam, Chef Steve says, "It's now unsinkable, but they said that about the *Titanic*, too!"

Eight months later, The Burger Boat launched in 2016 and has been a welcomed sight ever since. As the only one of its kind in Georgia, The Burger Boat is making waves in the food truck scene, serving 30 to 50 customers a day and even offering delivery to boaters on little barrier islands and beaches. Ticket times run 8 to 12 minutes. Find The Burger Boat at lunchtime by following @TheBurgerBoatSAV on Facebook or Instagram.

315-406-0804

LOVE'S SEAFOOD & STEAKS

A family business for four generations

A visit to Love's Seafood & Steaks wouldn't be complete without catching a colorful sunset while relaxing in the swing that faces the Ogeechee River. The restaurant sits along the banks of the 294-mile wide-mouthed Georgia river, and while waiting for a table or after a satisfying seafood dinner, guests can meander over to the graveled riverbank to enjoy the water views. They may even spot a manatee or wild alligator.

Family owned since 1949, Love's Seafood & Steaks is one of the few waterfront dining spots and is among the oldest established restaurants in Savannah. They are known for the recipe that started it all, their famous bone-in fried catfish dinner, which is sourced straight from the Ogeechee River and caught by the Love family themselves. Their most popular dishes include fried or grilled shrimp, oysters Rockefeller, and stuffed flounder, and while you're not guaranteed to see an alligator on the riverbanks, you'll definitely see one on the menu. Alligator fingers, otherwise known as fried gator tail, are served with a creamy peppercorn sauce.

Drive by on any afternoon or evening Thursday through Sunday, and the covered, pet-friendly deck, complete with ceiling fans, is packed with happy diners. Inside, a mix of tables and booths sit on hardwood floors next to large, oval-shaped picture windows reminiscent of the

In October of 1993, Love's Seafood & Steaks was selected by Paramount Pictures as one of the many filming locations of the Academy Award-Winning movie *Forrest Gump* starring Tom Hanks and Robin Wright.

Top left: Love's Seafood & Steaks has a large, covered patio for dining alfresco, which is also pet friendly. Photo courtesy of Love's Seafood & Steaks. *Above left:* Blackened Atlantic sea scallops are served with hush puppies and your choice of two sides. *Top center:* Fried catfish with handcut french fries are among the most popular dishes. Photo courtesy of Love's Seafood & Steaks. *Above center:* A pink and blue sunset on display over the Ogeechee River in full view of the diners. Photo courtesy of Love's Seafood & Steaks. *Top right:* Rest in the swing sets along the riverbank to enjoy the view. Photo courtesy of Love's Seafood & Steaks. *Above right:* Hot, crispy calamari topped with sliced banana peppers are a satisfying appetizer.

interior of a ship. A full bar is located behind the hostess stand with a big-screen TV to welcome football fans, and you'll find cocktails featuring locally sourced ingredients such as Savannah Bee Company honey. Be sure to leave room for dessert; classic homemade pies like Key lime, pecan, and apple will tempt your taste buds.

Of Love's Seafood & Steaks's many unique qualities, the service stands out. Servers are friendly, attentive, and knowledgeable. Let's be honest—you just don't find that everywhere. One of the most convenient things about dining at Love's is the large, gravel parking area. No downtown parking decks or parallel parking woes here.

Coastal Living magazine has named this special place a Top 25 Seafood Dive in several issues, and the restaurant has received many best-seafood and local people's choice awards. Just 20 minutes from downtown Savannah by way of I-16 and I-95, Love's Seafood is a must-visit destination.

6817 Chief of Love Rd.
912-925-3616, lovesseafood.com

BAKER'S PRIDE

Get your buns in here!

Baker's Pride is a name synonymous with delicious in Savannah. For more than 40 years, this family bakery has delighted locals and visitors alike with mouthwatering handmade cakes, doughnuts, and treats for Savannah and the Coastal Empire. From wedding cakes to pastries and chocolate chewies, everything in the tempting display case is baked on-site and made fresh daily.

Native to Savannah, the Baker family saw a need for a local bakery in their hometown, and so it began in 1982 as a small 1,200-square-foot corner store located at 5206 Waters Avenue. Back then, there was only room for two tables in the space. "My grandmother would have to fold bakery boxes at one of the two tables," says Trisha Lang, wedding consultant and co-owner. "The customers had to sit with her."

Today, that small corner store has expanded into a storefront of its own, more than doubling in size, and is located in a strip mall off of DeRenne Avenue, one of Savannah's busiest streets. "My son started kindergarten that year," says Trisha. "The Clothes Tree was next store, and we took in their retail area for customers to sit down. It allowed us to add a coffee station, juice and milk, drink machines, seating for customers, and an extra display." The 2,400-square-foot space now includes a dining area, a full product display, and a large production area for the bakery's wholesale clients and daily patrons.

Operated by Joella Baker and her daughters, Baker's Pride supports many well-known local restaurants, such as The Pirates' House, Clarey's, and Six Pence Pub, providing signature desserts and buns or rolls. Four days a week they make deliveries to nearby Hilton Head, South Carolina, and daily trips at various times

Top left: Baking cases are filled with an assortment of homemade doughnuts, Danishes, turnovers, and lemon bars. *Above left:* The inside of Baker's Pride is decorated for Valentine's Day, a popular holiday for the business. *Top right:* Baker's Pride is located on the end of an unassuming strip mall in Kensington Shopping Center off Derenne Avenue in Savannah. *Above right:* A bakery box of goodies including cream- and lemon-meringue-filled mini-doughnuts, cheese straws, red velvet and carrot cupcakes, and peanut butter cookies.

throughout the morning to support other community businesses such as corporations, universities, hospitals, and hotels.

Running a family business is a team effort. "We're all there every day," says Trisha. "We work a lot of hours doing whatever needs to be done." A popular doughnut chain recently closed its doors in Savannah, and since then, Baker's Pride has seen an uptick in business. Trisha says the difference in their doughnuts is that each one is hand cut using a doughnut cutter and produced one at a time. "Baker's Pride isn't a chain," she says. "It's a family name, and we bake with love."

840 E DeRenne Ave.
912-355-1155, savannahbakery.com

"We have always enjoyed being an asset to the community and seeing our customers get first birthday cakes all the way to their graduation and wedding cakes, and now bringing their own children by for sweets." –Trisha Lang, co-owner

CRYSTAL BEER PARLOR

Southern hospitality with history, charm and free-poured cocktails

A 1900s grocery-turned-restaurant, the Crystal Beer Parlor was once known as the Gerken Family Grocery Store. It was sold in the early 1930s to William "Blocko" and Connie Manning, who named it the Crystal, and it quickly gained a reputation as one of the first American eating establishments to serve alcohol after the repeal of Prohibition. Rumor has it that Mr. Blocko ran illegal hooch and operated a speakeasy during Prohibition.

Back then and still today, guests come for the juicy hamburgers, homemade fries, creamy crab stew, and hard-to-find beers on tap, made with rare ingredients. In a place called the Crystal Beer Parlor, you'll find an extended bar with ample seating. The bartenders here free-pour all cocktails, making the drinks just the way you like them. Welcoming high-top tables and booths invite guests to linger and enjoy Southern classic dishes like fried green tomatoes, shrimp and grits, and deviled crab. The food, including homemade sauces and salad dressings, is made from scratch daily. The Crystal Beer Parlor is known for its Savannah red rice, a defining dish of the Georgia coast; the pilaf is made with long-grain rice, which simmers in a seasoned broth until flavorful, getting its red color from acidic tomatoes.

Located in the Historic District at the intersection of Jones and Jefferson Streets, this red brick building has black window awnings and two entrances. You can walk directly into the bar from the sidewalk entrance or visit the main entrance near the gift shop to provide your name at the hostess stand.

The restaurant's walls are filled with black-and-white photographs that tell the story of the Crystal Beer Parlor and depict scenes

Left: With ample bar seating, the Crystal Beer Parlor offers more than 26 beers on tap. *Center left:* The Lamb Burger with charbroiled ground lamb and beef, homemade tzatziki sauce, lettuce, tomato, and onion. *Center right:* The Crystal Beer Parlor was established in 1933 and remains a Savannah favorite today. *Right:* Sentimental relics are displayed on the walls, such as this ice cream scoop used by the owner's grandfather, Paul Rousakis.

from Savannah's past, including some of the city's most famous and infamous citizens. The legend lives on in pictures of former waiters like Monroe Whitlock and A. G. "Smitty" Smith, who were restaurant servers here for almost 45 years.

Three large menu boards, original to the Crystal, have been preserved and mounted on wood, and they now hang proudly in the Smitty room, lovingly named for Mr. Smith. Many of those same menu items are still served today. A casual yet elevated dining experience, here you'll experience knowledgeable, efficient servers and friendly Southern hospitality in a historic beer parlor setting.

301 W Jones St.
912-349-1000, crystalbeerparlor.com

Restaurant owner John Nichols has a rich family heritage in Savannah and comes from a long line of entrepreneurs and restaurateurs. Both of his grandfathers owned and operated food businesses, including the Lunch Room on West Broad Street, (now Martin Luther King Jr. Boulevard) and Paul's Soda Shop on Bull and Maupas Streets. The ice cream scoop Paul Rousakis used from 1930 to 1955 is proudly displayed as wall art today.

SAVANNAH SEAFOOD SHACK

Fast-casual local seafood

David and Christine Cutlip got the idea to open the Savannah Seafood Shack on their honeymoon in Thailand in what Christine calls "the sea-to-table experience," where they ate at every dive and hole-in-the-wall restaurant to get the true local experience. Inspired and ready to start a new adventure, they opened the Savannah Seafood Shack (where Christina's dad is the chef), on popular Broughton Street, one of the city's most bustling shopping and dining areas.

Starting a seafood business was second nature to founder and CEO Christine. Her parents own a local seafood market in nearby Pooler, where they sell fresh shrimp, crab, and fish. Her family has been in the seafood business for more than 25 years.

Christine was eight months pregnant when the location for the Savannah Seafood Shack became available. Her bun in the oven was the inspiration for one of the restaurant's most popular menu items, the Love Shack. It's a Low Country Boil loaded with 18 local shrimp, smoked beef sausage, and crab legs, finished with a squeeze of lemon, garlic butter, and a blend of secret in-house Cajun spices. Served up in a single-person portion bag for a mess-free meal, they

Visiting Savannah but don't feel like leaving the comfort of your room? Order online or have your meal delivered! Savannah Seafood Shack proudly partners with DoorDash and Uber Eats, and offers in-store pickup. Indoor and outdoor seating is available, but they do not take reservations.

Left: Steamin' Combos are boiled and steamed with house Cajun seasoning, topped with lemon and garlic butter and served with potatoes and corn on the cob. *Center:* Christina Cutlip, founder and CEO. *Top right:* Shack Cones feature a homemade waffle cone, filled with creamy coleslaw, topped with your choice of protein and Shack sauce. *Above right:* The interior of Savannah Seafood Shack reflects its coastal locale. All photos courtesy of Savannah Seafood Shack.

say once you eat this dish, you're sure to be in love. You can even upgrade by ordering your shrimp peeled and deveined.

Another menu item that makes the Savannah Seafood Shack unique is the Shack Cone. Made-from-scratch waffle cones are layered with your choice of fried shrimp, fish, calamari, oysters, or even chicken tenders, with a lightly dressed house-made slaw. They say it's better than ice cream, because it doesn't melt!

The interior of the restaurant transports you to the coast, with crab nets and starfish adorning the wood-planked walls and large prints of brightly framed seafood dishes. One long bench seat runs the wall of the restaurant, creating multiple tables topped with salt and pepper shakers, cocktail sauce, ketchup, and much-needed paper towel rolls. Place your order at a walk-up counter and your meal will be delivered swiftly to your table.

Featured on the Cooking Channel, the Travel Channel, and the Food Network, the Savannah Seafood Shack earns its Low Country eats and fried-tastic reputation honestly.

116 E Broughton St.
912-344-4393, savannahseafoodshack.com

MRS. WILKES' DINING ROOM

Southern comfort food family style since 1943

The legendary Mrs. Sema Wilkes of Toombs County, Georgia, learned to cook when she was just 7 years old. "They'd tell her how to pull a chair up to the stove and cook with the farmhands," says Marcia Thompson, Mrs. Wilkes's granddaughter. After losing both of her parents by the age of 12, Mrs. Wilkes married at the tender age of 16, and due to unforeseen circumstances, she and her new husband moved to Savannah. Little did she know it would be that very same skill set—cooking—that would take her and her family around the world, provide a family business for generations, and make her a household name.

Soon after Mrs. Wilkes married Lois Herman Wilkes in the 1920s, the couple experienced several hardships. "As soon as they married, they had the Spanish flu, so they almost died, then there was the Depression, and the farm was taken by eminent domain to build an airfield, and that's how we got here," says Marcia. "They had to pick up and leave everything they'd ever known."

The couple moved to Savannah in the early 1940s and settled at Mrs. Dennis Dixon's Boardinghouse, where the young bride began working. Three years later, she and her husband bought the boardinghouse and renamed it Mrs. Wilkes' Dining Room, which quickly became and remains a Savannah institution. Mrs. Wilkes lived to be 95 years old and worked in her restaurant every day that she was able, until she passed away in 2002.

Mrs. Wilkes' is known for its crispy fried chicken and melt-in-your-mouth biscuits, and the midday meal is served daily family style with more than 20 bowls of vegetables. Oval dining tables covered

Left: Platters of crispy fried chicken, white rice, Savannah red rice, corn bread, and sweet tea. *Center left:* You can still stay at Mrs. Wilkes' Dining Room, a convenient walk to many downtown attractions. *Center right:* Marcia Thompson, Mrs. Wilkes's granddaughter, carries on the tradition of Southern hospitality. *Right:* Mrs. Sema Wilkes displays her "Distinguished Restaurant Award" from *Conde Nast Traveler*, 1990. Photo courtesy of John Carrington for *Savannah Morning News.*

in white tablecloths are filled with collard greens flavored with ham hock, fried okra, red rice, and cold peppered cucumbers. "I think sitting with people from all over the world is special; there's something about eating food together that changes the whole dynamic," says Marcia.

When the table is set and eager diners are seated, Marcia will offer the grace before the meal—"Good Lord, bless this food to us, and us to thy service"—just as Mrs. Wilkes did for 59 years.

"You know what they say—that the biggest factor for longevity is how many people you meet every day, and maybe that's why Mrs. Wilkes lived to be 95," says Marcia. "People today still tell me how kind and gentle she was with them, and how she was always interested in what they were eating."

107 W Jones St.
mrswilkes.com

Mrs. Wilkes' Dining Room received the James Beard Foundation America's Regional Classics Award, given to locally owned restaurants that have timeless appeal and are beloved regionally for quality food that reflects the character of its community. Remember, it's one menu, one price, and cash only. No booze, but plenty of sweet tea to go around.

OGEECHEE MEAT MARKET

Staying ahead of the game with old-fashioned service

Gary and Robin McClune met as high schoolers working at a grocery store chain in their hometown of Gettysburg, Pennsylvania. Gary, a meat apprentice, worked in the back, and Robin, a cashier, ran the front end of the grocery store. The couple married and had two sons, Matthew and Andrew, and today, together with their boys, they own and operate Ogeechee Meat Market, an award-winning, old-fashioned, full-service butcher shop best known for its one-on-one customer service and more than 28 different flavors of sausage.

"My great grandfather was a butcher, and being in the meat business was just something I always wanted to do," says Gary. "When I was 16 years old working in the grocery business, I was always intrigued by the guys in the back cutting meat."

Gary has more than 50 years of experience, and has taught both of his sons the tricks of the trade. In addition to cutting meat, Matthew and Andrew each bring their own talents to the family business. Matthew is in charge of smoking meats, a process of exposing food to smoke to preserve, brown, or add flavor. From Boston butts and ribs to corned beef brisket for St. Patrick's Day and turkeys at Thanksgiving, Robin says, "He'll smoke anything once." Andrew specializes in putting meals together to offer customers an

Ogeechee Meat Market's Vidalia Onion Sausage won first place in the 2014 Flavor of Georgia Food Product Contest sponsored by the University of Georgia Center for Agribusiness and Economic Development. Try their homemade sausage–it's the bestseller!

Top left: The meat case holds freshly butchered filet mignons, rib eye steaks, and more. You can also order whole cases and loins of meat. *Above left:* The McClune family (clockwise from left): Matt and his brother Andrew. Seated: Robin and Gary McClune. *Top right:* The new Ogeechee Meat Market barn under construction in December 2023. *Above right:* Jars of homemade jams and fresh fruit preserves line the wooden shelves. Barbecue sauces, steak sauces, and seasonings are also available.

economical packaged option. "My family has helped me achieve what I've wanted to achieve," says Gary.

Gary and Robin understand the value and importance of preserving the traditional butcher shop because it's something from the past that needs to be maintained. "People appreciate it," says Gary, "and they like people who are knowledgeable about what they are selling." Customers also like the ability to customize the thickness of their steak.

Over the years, Gary has seen the industry evolve. From the early 1970s compared to today, he says it is overwhelming how fast things have changed. Today the market demands convenience, and to be successful the McClunes have learned they must be willing to pivot and must always stay one step ahead. During the COVID-19 pandemic, the McClunes didn't close for a single day. Instead, they transitioned to strictly drive-through. "You've got to change, and that's where my family has done a great job," says Gary.

In the coming months, the McClunes are expanding their offerings to include fresh vegetables and will move the 20-year-old business next door, where they are turning it into a big red barn, so no one will miss it. "I don't know what kind of produce man I am," said Gary, "but we're going to try!"

6021 Ogeechee Rd.
912-961-5223, ogeecheemeatmarket.com

KAYAK KAFÉ

A healthy oasis in the land of Southern cooking

Brendan Pappas, a native of Tybee Island, Georgia, and Monique Silen of Panama, met while Monique was a graduate student studying at the Savannah College of Art and Design. It was her friend and roommate who introduced the couple, and they would later marry and build a thriving business together with a menu inspired by their travels and a passion for fast-casual food that's both health conscious and fresh.

With two locations, one in the heart of Savannah's Historic District and one in the city's Midtown Medical Arts Community, Kayak Kafé has been in business for more than 17 years. It all started in the downtown location as part of a gym, serving smoothies and healthy bites, but over the years it has evolved organically into a two-part vision focusing on consistent, quality food and service that has served the restaurant and its community well. "Two of our most popular salads are our Mexican chicken salad and the Broughton Cobb," said Monique, co-owner of Kayak Kafé. "If someone comes here and they are craving the Broughton Cobb salad, I want it to be the same way, perfect, every time they come." That consistency is what makes Kayak Kafé what it is, and what keeps the customers coming back again and again.

In the restaurant industry, staffing and finding the right candidate can be the biggest challenge. "For us, it's been so important that whomever we bring in and hire, we want this to become their career and home for a long time," says Monique. And they're well on their

Kayak Kafé is consistently rated the best place in town for fresh salads, gluten-free options, and vegetarian and vegan cuisine. Healthy eats for every dietary style!

Left: Clockwise from top: Broughton Cobb, harvest lentil burger, vegan taco bowl, Wild Georgia shrimp and avocado quesadilla, vegetarian salad, spicy jerk chicken tacos. Photo courtesy of Siobhan Egan for Paprika Southern. *Center:* Husband-and-wife duo Monique Silen (left) and Brendan Pappas (right), owner and operators of Kayak Kafé, celebrate the two-year anniversary of the midtown location in 2015. Photo courtesy of Kayak Kafé. *Right:* Broughton Cobb. Photo courtesy of Siobhan Egan for Paprika Southern.

way to achieving that goal. More than 50 percent of Kayak Kafé's staff have been with the company for nearly seven years.

Throughout the years, Monique says they've learned and evolved. "It's a continuous thing," she says. "We've been through two recessions and the pandemic. We know who we are and we don't want to change that. We don't want to be anything different."

That confidence carries over in everything the Kayak Kafé brand stands for: wholesome food that tastes good and is made fresh daily with no preservatives, artificial flavors, or colors and Green To-Go 100 percent compostable eco-products.

While the menu may be healthy, it also includes items everyone loves, such as sweet potato fries, crinkle-cut fries, and chicken wings. "That has been our jam when it comes to making everyone happy," says Monique. "The whole thing is that we cater to all diets, so there's going to be a little something for everyone."

Kayak Downtown
1 E Broughton St.
912-233-6044

Kayak Midtown
5002 Paulsen St. (@ 66th)
912-349-4371

eatkayak.com

THE BAMBOO ROOM TIKI BAR

A tropical hideaway

If you want to be transported to a Polynesian paradise, look no further. Nestled on the second floor of Sorry Charlie's Oyster Bar & Cocktails is the Bamboo Room Tiki Bar, a tropical oasis unlike anything else in the city. With classic tiki and modern cocktails, an island-inspired menu true to its Southern locale, and a menagerie of artifacts collected by its six business partners from around the globe, this island getaway adds something different to the Savannah landscape.

When dreaming up the concept for this intimate space with its own mystique, the ownership team was intentional about diving into tiki culture, spending months traveling across the country to visit iconic tiki bars such as San Francisco's Tonga Room & Hurricane Bar and Archipelago in Washington, DC. Step through the more-than-500-year-old fertility doors and be immediately enchanted by the enormous, hand-carved wooden tiki gods anchoring the horseshoe-shaped bar. Take in the shrunken heads from the ancient Jivaroan Tribes of Southern Ecuador and the brightly colored globes and lanterns wrapped in fishing nets adorning the ceiling.

With the most extensive rum selection in Savannah, the menu features made-to-order tropical cocktails and frozen drinks made using fresh juices, premium spirits, and house-made syrups. Some concoctions boast 15 components and strike the perfect balance of spice and fruit. Creativity shines in the cocktails, mugs, and decor.

Much of the rum is aged in bourbon barrels, like the Martinique Rhum J.M, a single-batch reserve chosen for its distinctive notes of grilled fruit and toasted vanilla bean influenced by American oak.

Top left: Prepare to experience delicious tiki cocktails, frozen drinks, island-inspired snacks, friendly people, and funky vibes. *Above left:* Blue Hawaiian, made with vodka, blue curaçao, lemon, pineapple, and coconut. *Top right:* A Coy Decoy, made with gin, grapefruit, pineapple, bitters, and lime. *Above right:* The Devil You Know, made with tequila, mezcal, brandy, orgeat, mango, pineapple, lime, and bitters. All photos courtesy of Sorry Charlie's.

Bartender Melanie Heider says, "I feel like people are afraid of rums because they think Captain Morgan, sweet coconut, or Malibu, but rums are so diverse." In addition to the more than 200 bottles of rum, you can try a variety of flavor profiles with bourbon, tequila, or vodka.

Whether you're on vacation or looking for a romantic hideaway with your special someone, the Bamboo Room Tiki Bar offers a fun and lively atmosphere with something for everyone, including oysters and crab fries.

"It's just a special place where you come and you want to have a good time," says Melanie. "I feel like you can't walk in here and be upset. Hopefully you get your drink, you get a really cool mug, you taste it, you love it, and you say, 'Alright, today wasn't so bad because of this.'"

116 W Congress St.
912-234-5397, bamboorоomtikibar.com

Sorry Charlie's Oyster Bar & Cocktails was named to *Southern Living*'s Top 5 Local Restaurants in Georgia in the South's Best awards for 2023.

HUSK RESTAURANT

Expand your palate and curiosity

Consider the word *husk*. It is literally the outer covering of a seed, fruit, or vegetable, but for HUSK Restaurant in Savannah, the word means something deeper. "The significance of the name comes from wanting to protect Southern ingredients, techniques, and farmers growing specific breeds of livestock or strains of produce, because they are so special if used correctly," says General Manager Joshua Gause.

Housed in a Southern mansion in Savannah's Landmark Historic District, HUSK is a seasonally driven eatery celebrating Southern ingredients and exploring the foodways of coastal Georgia. Executive Chef and Savannah native Chris Hathcock designs menus daily with Japanese and coastal Georgia influences that highlight the bounty of local farmers and feature dishes with distinct Southern identity.

"We are here to highlight what the city of Savannah and its neighboring outskirts have to offer in the way of produce and ocean life," says Joshua. "Our goal is to not just be a business ourselves, but to build up the smaller businesses we get our product from on a daily basis."

Sourced from the South, HUSK's ingredient-forward cuisine is modern in style and interpretation. Take the three-tier fresh seafood tower served with sea-salted blini featuring a selection of raw oysters, seasonal raw fish crudos, peel-and-eat shrimp, and caviar.

The Neighborhood Dining Group (NDG) is led by President David Howard, a James Beard semifinalist for Best Restaurateur. NDG has earned many accolades, including *Bon Appétit* magazine's "Best New Restaurant in America" for HUSK Charleston, and for HUSK Nashville, *GQ*'s "12 Most Outstanding Restaurants of the Year," and *Esquire*'s "Best New Restaurant in America."

Left: Tuna sashimi, daikon radish, sea beans. *Center left:* Chef Chris Hathcock prepares fresh tortellini with egg dough. *Center right:* Strawberry shortcake, fermented honey, biscuit streusel, vanilla bean. *Right:* Joshua Gause, General Manager at HUSK. All photos courtesy of HUSK and Andrew Lee.

Layered within the crushed ice you may find bright green, crunchy, salty sea beans, which slightly resemble thin asparagus with multiple shoots. Don't mistake these for a garnish. They're actually grown in Charleston and sourced from the region's first saltwater hydroponics farm. Unique accompaniments such as cold horseradish-peanut relish are included for topping oysters.

"The seafood tower highlights what sets HUSK Savannah apart from the other HUSKS, which are our raw bar options," says Joshua. "It gives you an introduction to almost everything we do at the raw bar, in a really fun showstopper way."

With three locations in Savannah, Charleston, and Nashville, HUSK is part of the Neighborhood Dining Group portfolio of restaurants including Minero in Atlanta; Minero Mexican Grill & Cantina in Johns Island, South Carolina; and Delany Oyster Bar in Charleston.

When it comes to what to order, Joshua challenges guests to think outside the box. "If you love shrimp and you know you love shrimp, maybe don't order shrimp," he says. "Try one of our cured fish crudos or tuna sashimi instead that highlights not only our supplier but the fish itself. Let your curiosity and spontaneous side guide your decisions, not your comfort or hunger."

12 W Oglethorpe Ave.
912-349-2600, husksavannah.com

THE PIRATES' HOUSE

A Savannah treasure

In what was formerly an inn and tavern for pirates and sailors from the seven seas now sits The Pirates' House, a world-famous seafood restaurant known for its daily Southern luncheon buffet, award-winning honey-pecan fried chicken, and soul-satisfying seafood. The Pirates' House is the largest restaurant in Savannah, complete with 14 unique dining rooms and a second-floor gift shop with all the loot you can imagine.

Situated just a block from the Savannah River in what is considered the oldest standing building in Georgia, the restaurant is easily recognizable with its haint-blue shutters and doors said to keep unwanted spirits away. Before it was an inn, this site was the Trustee's Garden, the first agricultural, experimental garden in America developed by General James Oglethorpe four months after arriving ashore. In 1734 the Herb House was constructed to house the gardener of the Trustee's Garden. Later, in the mid-1700s, when Savannah became a thriving seaport town, the Herb House was expanded to an inn and tavern that provided many tales about those who came through its doors.

Legend has it that multiple tunnels below the building led back to the Savannah River, and that pirates would use the tunnels to capture unsuspecting men to stock their ship's crew. One famous tale includes a local police officer who stopped by The Pirates' House for a drink and

Treasure Island, a novel written by Scottish author Robert Louis Stevenson circa 1883, mentions The Pirates' House in Savannah and a pirate by the name of Captain John Flint. It is said that Stevenson was inspired to write the tale while visiting the inn, and early-edition pages can be found in the Treasure Room today.

Top left: The Savannah crab dip appetizer is warm with a blend of crabmeat, cheese, horseradish, and spices, served with toasted pita points. *Above left:* The Pirates' House has 14 unique dining rooms, each with a personality all its own. *Top center:* Order a featured cocktail from the full bar, such as the Skull Crusher, with light and dark rum, cranberry, pineapple and orange juices, plus a float of 151 rum. *Above center:* The seafood harvest platter entrée comes with shrimp, oysters, and fish, lightly breaded and deep fried, served with french fries. *Right:* The Pirates' House most precious treasure is the food. All photos courtesy of The Pirates' House.

awoke on a four-masted schooner sailing to China. They say it took him two years to make his way back to Savannah. Shiver me timbers!

In 1945, the property and the dilapidated building were slated for demolition, but Mrs. Mary Hillyer recognized its historical significance and saw the potential no one else did. Mary was the wife of Savannah Gas Company president Hansell Hillyer. Determined and talented, with the help of other local women Mary led the historic preservation efforts, obtaining approval to renovate the area. The seven-year project was a success, which led to the opening of The Pirates' House tearoom in 1953 by Herbert Smith Traub Jr. and his business partner James T. Casey. Herbert grew The Pirates' House into worldwide fame, establishing it as a family-friendly destination that would provide memories and rousing good times for years to come.

Today, the restaurant's rich history draws locals and tourists from around the world. Whether you visit in hopes of seeing a ghost or for the bounty of delicious food and drink, this Savannah institution is a treasure worth the adventure.

20 E Broad St.
912-233-5757, thepirateshouse.com

ERICA DAVIS LOWCOUNTRY

Where fresh Savannah seafood still exists

Erica Russo Davis is a well-known caterer, but since October of 2019 she and her husband, Dwight, have been what they've deemed "accidental restaurateurs." Call it an accident or fate, but serving fresh Savannah seafood was always in the cards for Erica. It's in her blood.

Erica comes from a family that knows seafood. Her paternal grandfather was the late Charles Joseph Russo Sr., who began Russo's Seafood Market in 1946. It remains a thriving business in Savannah to this day. Vincent Russo, Erica's father, worked in the family's seafood market for many years, but eventually broke away from it to start his own catering company. Erica started working alongside her dad when she was 15 years old, and after college she started catering full-time. "I didn't think I would be in the seafood business at all—my background was in recreation therapy, so it was never supposed to be," she says. "But it's funny how we did it on the side and it just kind of built up."

And build up it has. Erica Davis Lowcountry is located in the small fishing village of Thunderbolt, Georgia, in a former gas station turned seafood restaurant. She and Dwight renovated the building, giving it a total overhaul, but the couple's original intention was to use the space as a catering kitchen and venue for small parties, like bridal showers and rehearsal dinners. "When COVID hit, we started selling takeouts to get revenue going, and then that became a restaurant," says Dwight. An industrial engineer, Dwight grew up in his Southern mother's kitchen learning to cook and now helps with a great deal of the catering, while Erica focuses her attention on the restaurant. When the opportunity presented itself to renovate the space, Dwight told Erica, "This is my Taj Mahal to you."

Left: Roasted oysters, collards and cream, Parmesan. *Center:* Wassaw redfish with pan-seared redfish fillets, garlic beurre blanc, heirloom tomato, stone-ground grits, and fresh green beans. *Right:* Erica and Dwight Davis, owners. All photos courtesy of Erica Davis Lowcountry.

Part of the impetus behind starting the restaurant was the need to answer one question everyone seemed to ask: Where do you go for good seafood? "There was always this hesitation of 'Do I want to send them there, because they use Chinese shrimp,'" says Dwight. "Savannah seafood is not crab legs from Alaska. That's Alaskan seafood." The couple knew they could fill that void.

Erica Davis Lowcountry specializes in fresh, local ingredients, quality food, and great service, making 98 percent of their cuisine from scratch. The Southern, coastal menu is a true taste of Savannah, bringing together seafood, barbecue, chicken, ribs, brisket, and delectable Southern sides.

3209 E Victory Dr.
912-544-5544, ericadavislowcountry.com

Erica Davis Lowcountry earned recognition in 2023 on the Bulldog 100, a list of the top 100 fastest-growing organizations owned or operated by University of Georgia alumni.

BIG BON BODEGA

Bagels and wood-fired pizza with purpose

At the corner of West 37th and Bull Streets in the Starland District, otherwise known as Savannah's most eclectic neighborhood, is Big Bon Bodega, a bagel and pizza shop that's serving more than great food. Owned by Kay Heritage, a South Korean native who has called the Hostess City home for more than 33 years, Big Bon Bodega's purpose is to teach its team members business and life skills while instilling in them core values such as respect, kindness, and love for community.

Today you can't miss the large, black-and-white Art Deco building, once a service station, painted with red letters and a crown positioned high above the front door. But Big Bon Bodega didn't begin as a brick and mortar.

"We started as a food truck in 2016," says Kay. "My daughter and I thought it would be super cool to have a massive, Italian, Neapolitan pizza oven on the back of a trailer and just go around serving pizza, and it turned out to be a really fun experience for Savannah, because we didn't have anything like that." Neapolitan-style pizza has a different dough hydration, known for being very tender, light, and moist, and abides by the principle that less is more when it comes to ingredients.

After building a large following and fan base with the food truck, they launched the bagel shop three years later. The menu features bagel sandwiches such as the popular 912, which makes up 60 percent of their sandwich sales. It's served on an everything bagel with crispy

In 2023, Big Bon Bodega was featured on two national TV shows: *Samantha Brown's Places to Love* on PBS and Guy Fieri's *Diners, Drive-Ins and Dives* on Food Network.

Top: Big Bon Bodega's firstborn child on wheels, the wood-fired pizza trailer has catered more than 500 weddings, corporate events, birthday parties, and graduations. *Above left:* Stephanie Izard, Kay Heritage, and Guy Fieri (left to right) outside Big Bon Bodega during the filming of *Diners, Drive-Ins and Dives* on Food Network. *Above right:* Anna Heritage, Kay's daughter, enjoys the sesame seed bagel filled with cream cheese. All photos courtesy of Big Bon Bodega.

bacon, egg, two cheeses, and herb butter. You can also choose from seven different bagel flavors, and all the spreads—including kimchi, scallion and herb, and a vegan option—made in-house.

Big Bon Bodega is lovingly named in honor of Kay's husband, Kevin, an alumni of Texas A&M University and proud Aggie who loves bonfires and hosts them often at their home in the country, inviting friends and family to come and sit around the fire.

Much like a bonfire in its ability to bring people together, Big Bon Bodega has become a gathering place where people come first and profit follows. "Becoming rich is not my goal," says Kay. "What's exciting for me is using this tool—bagels—to really provide great jobs and impact some people. If we can do that, it's all good."

2011 Bull St.
912-349-4847, bigbonfamily.com

CHARLES J. RUSSO'S SEAFOOD

Providing fresh, quality seafood since 1946

In 1946, shortly after returning home from World War II, Charles Joseph Russo Sr. and his wife, Antoinette, opened Russo's Seafood at the corner of 31st Street and Waters Avenue. Originally born in Maynard, Massachusetts, Charles came to Savannah with his family by way of a boat with the intention to settle in Jacksonville, Florida; luckily for Savannahians, the boat's last stop was Savannah.

"There were eight children," Charles J. Russo Jr. (Charlie), owner of Russo's Seafood, told YouTube's *Our City Host*. "They couldn't take the cold weather, so they put the truck, the kids, and my grandmother on the boat, and Savannah was the last stop."

Charles Sr. was employed with the US Post Office at the time, but he had worked in the seafood business during the Great Depression and had maintained an interest in it. His wife's family also had a thriving seafood business in Savannah, named after his mother-in-law, Mrs. A. C. Mathews, who offered to loan the couple money to help them start their own business.

The Russos spent 24 years in that first location, and in June of 1970, they opened a new, more modern, and larger market on West 40th Street, where they've been a fixture in the community ever since. Over the years, local customers and tourists have come to rely on Russo's Seafood for the highest-quality cut-to-order fresh fish, fresh and frozen local shrimp, scallops, oysters, clams, mussels, live crab, soft-shell blue crab, and much more.

Not only do they sell fresh seafood, but they also have "extras," as Charlie likes to call them, such as potato salad, deviled crab, crab

Left: Charlie J. Russo Jr., owner. Photo courtesy of Cecilia Russo Marketing. *Center:* Fresh shucked oysters on the half shell with cocktail sauce, lemon, and parsley. *Right:* Inside the fish market, Ulises, an employee, stocks fresh-caught sea bass on ice.

stew, and coleslaw. Stop in for convenient ready-to-eat items you can pick up fresh off the ice, such as a dozen raw oysters on the half shell served with a lemon wedge and homemade cocktail sauce.

In 1984, *Vincent Russo's Seafood Cookbook* was published with a dedication to his parents: "To my mother and father who worked so hard to provide for their family and in doing so, saw their business prosper."

With more than 75 years in business, the Russo family has prided itself on offering the very best seafood prepared in the cleanest and most sanitary surroundings in the Southeast, and they're not slowing down anytime soon. "So many people ask me when I'm going to retire, but I don't plan on it," says Charlie. "The enjoyment of it keeps me going."

201 E 40th St.
912-234-5196

246 Red Cedar St., Bluffton, SC
843-837-7000

In the summer of 2019, Charles Russo III opened Russo's Seafood in Bluffton, South Carolina, as a production facility and wholesale market providing fresh fish to several area restaurants. Three generations of fishmongers!

SANDFLY BAR-B-Q

Memphis born, Savannah made

A colorful, wall-sized chalkboard menu—along with the smell of smoked sausage, slow-cooked pulled pork, and simmering Brunswick stew—greet you as you step inside Sandfly Bar-B-Q. Located in the quaint community of Sandfly in the historic Newton's Corner shopping center, this popular barbecue joint is known for what owner Keith Latture likes to call "Savannah-style barbecue," traditionally seasoned and smoked over a combination of pecan and hickory woods.

Complete with clapboard walls of chipped paint and bright red booths, the restaurant's down-home, genuine atmosphere welcomes hungry patrons from near and far. In the small eat-in dining room, a buck head is mounted on the wall above the drink dispenser and strung with white Christmas lights year-round. You can also dine outside on the covered sidewalk at one of the ironclad tables or at the patriotic picnic table with paper towel rolls as centerpieces.

As a native of Memphis, Tennessee, Keith comes by his love of barbecue honestly. "Our barbecue is very similar to the kind of barbecue I grew up eating in Memphis, which is a very distinct style, but we cater our sides and sauces to the Savannah market," he shared, in a Savannah Small Business Assistance Corporation spotlight video on YouTube.

Regular sides are available by the pint and quart and include coleslaw, baked beans, collards, green beans, potato salad, and mac and cheese—not to mention the crispy, hand-cut french fries and cold sweet tea. "Our sides are a reflection of what we learned growing up in the South; we make them how our grandparents did," says Keith. "We take pride in the simple things."

No barbecue joint is complete without its sauces, and as with most Southern barbecue establishments worth their weight, Sandfly Bar-B-Q's three distinct sauces are no exception. "Our sauces show off

Top left: Grab a seat in the welcoming dining area. *Above left:* All plates are served with two sides and Texas toast. Photo courtesy of Sandfly Bar-B-Q. *Top center:* For great variety, try three sliders featuring your choice of pork, brisket, chicken, or sausage. *Above center:* A chalkboard menu greets guests with daily specials. *Right:* Pulled pork is one of Sandfly Bar-B-Q's most popular dishes. Photo courtesy of Sandfly Bar-B-Q.

our regional travels," says Keith. Try them all—there's a Memphis-style sweet sauce; a zesty, mustard-based Savannah sauce; and a spicy, vinegar-based Western North Carolina sauce.

The late John "Butch" Keith Latture Sr. opened Sandfly Bar-B-Q in 2007 with nothing but a small smoker, a lot of talent, and a dream. Since then, the restaurant has been consistently recognized as one of the best barbecue restaurants in Savannah by the readers of *Connect Savannah* magazine. In 2022, Sandfly Bar-B-Q was voted Best of the Coastal Empire in the Official Community Choice Awards by *Savannah Morning News*.

As the saying goes, Sandfly Bar-B-Q is "Out Here—You Got That Right!"

8413 Ferguson Ave.
912-356-5463, sandflybbq.com

Sandfly Bar-B-Q offers full-service catering, takeout, and online ordering.

COHEN'S RETREAT

Art. Food. Community.

The majestic Savannah landmark built in 1934 as a nursing home for men, affectionately known as "The Cohen's Old Man's Retreat," today is a family destination for celebrating art, delicious food, and community, thanks to visionary and Savannah native Colleen Kaney Smith ("Co").

Co grew up on nearby Isle of Hope and has fond memories of visiting the men's home with her church youth group, singing and bringing gift baskets to the residents. She returned as a college student and recalls visiting with one gentleman who didn't have any family. "His name was John and he was from Connecticut," she says. "He loved art. I would come and bring my portfolio of what I had worked on in art class that day, and we would sit out there on those benches in the trees and spend time together."

Those same benches, now painted a bright orange, remain on the property with some positioned alongside the wrought-iron fence separating it from busy Skidaway Road. "The reason they're so close to the fence is because the little fellas put their feet there, up on the brick, and you would drive by in the afternoon, and they would be out there smoking like giants," she said chuckling, "waving their little flags." The memory of the gentlemen who once resided here is preserved through subtle nods in the eclectic interior design: brightly painted ashtrays, along with collections of walking canes, now serve as wall art; vintage aftershave bottles and mug brushes decorate mantels, but the decor isn't the only thing that's inspired.

Cohen's is open for brunch, lunch, and dinner, and the seasonal menus showcase upscale Lowcountry cuisine prepared by Chef David Landrigan—originally from upstate New York—who has cooked in many impressive Savannah restaurants for more than 15 years. "David has the whole package," says Co. "He just brings something

Left: Colleen K. Smith, founder of Cohen's Retreat. Photo courtesy of Kelli Boyd Photography. *Top center:* A large framed photo of Percival Randolph Cohen is proudly displayed above the mantel in the main dining room. Photo courtesy of Kelli Boyd Photography. *Above center:* Located in the Moon River District, just 20 minutes south of downtown, you can dine, shop, and stay at Cohen's Retreat. Book one of the 10 charming cottages. Photo courtesy of Kelli Boyd Photography. *Top right:* Try a popular à la carte side dish of fried brussels and bacon. *Above right:* The Southern tomato pie has a house-made crust and is filled with a blend of tomatoes, Vidalia onions, and fresh basil, topped with a balsamic reduction.

different to the table. He's very passionate, and he's artistic. You can't teach someone that." Chef David brings European influences to the Southern menu and enjoys helping others understand how to cook with accessible ingredients. What's more, thanks to Co's son Bo, Blue Heron Farms (five acres in neighboring Garden City) supplies all of the restaurant's vegetables.

After closing in the 1980s, the 13,000-square-foot building eventually fell into bankruptcy. "When I realized it was going to be auctioned off, I said, 'This is crazy, but what if?'" Co says. "What if we could create a space that the Savannah community could come together and enjoy?"

5715 Skidaway Rd.
912-355-3336, cohensretreat.com

The namesake of the building is Percival Randolph Cohen (1851–1927), a Savannah businessman and philanthropist who designated $50,000 in his will to "construct a facility where men would not die old and lonely." His portrait hangs above the mantel in the main dining room today.

PAULA DEEN'S THE LADY & SONS

Love and best dishes, y'all

In November of 2023, Paula Deen and her two sons, Jamie and Bobby, celebrated 20 years in their second downtown location of the Lady & Sons restaurant. The three-story building with 15,000 square feet of dining space seats nearly 330 hungry diners from around the globe daily, and it has become a world-renowned restaurant and full-service catering venue. The place is known for its endless portions of hearty entrées, including Paula's favorite chicken-fried pork chops, and down-home side dishes like mashed potatoes with gravy, and each meal ends with a mouthwatering dessert. But her journey thus far has not come without its challenges.

In 1989, at 42 years old with barely a high school education, Paula invested her last $200 to start her catering business, the Bag Lady. "I had to ask myself, 'Well, what's your talent, girl?'" she says. "Cooking food. So, I said, 'Okay, that'll be the lane I'm going to go in; so let's figure out how I can put that to work.'"

With a business license, $50 worth of groceries, and a cooler, Paula made lunches out of her home kitchen and sent her boys to sell them to local businesses. The Bag Lady business took off, and eventually Paula moved into the Best Western on the south side of Savannah, cooking the buffet. She spent five of what she describes as the hardest years of her life there, providing three meals a day, seven days a week, simultaneously maintaining her catering business.

In 1996, Paula opened the Lady & Sons in its first downtown location. By this time she had published two cookbooks and her popularity was growing—as was the line outside of her restaurant.

Left: The Lady & Sons is Paula's flagship restaurant located at the corner of Whitaker and Congress Streets in downtown Savannah. *Center:* In true Southern tradition, scratch cheese biscuits are served with every meal. *Top right:* Pass the plates, and try the beef pot roast or the Georgia fried catfish for a taste of comfort food at its finest! *Above right:* Paula, Jamie, Bobby, and Ineata Jones (clockwise from left) who goes by the nickname Jelly Roll. All photos courtesy of Kelli Boyd Photography.

Seven years passed, during which she earned international recognition and launched a national TV show.

Today, the Lady & Sons is one of Savannah's most charming places to dine. Lunch and dinner are served family style, but you sit with the individuals with whom you arrived. You can find Jamie in the restaurant's newest addition, the Chicken Box, at 106 W. Julian Street, offering delicious on-the-go lunch options.

Now in her late 70s, Paula is the picture of resilience and attributes much of her success to her sons. "I couldn't have done it without them," she says. Her story is one of survival, and her empire is built on hard work, long hours, and consistency. "I thank God every day for my sense of humor," Paula says. "And I genuinely love people."

102 W Congress St.
912-233-2600, ladyandsons.com

Parking for the Lady & Sons restaurant is all on-street parking. The meters are free after 8 p.m. on weekdays and Saturdays, and all day on Sundays. No need to make a reservation.

BAOBAB LOUNGE

Trading the Finest Provisions from Savanna to Savannah

When you think of Savannah, you may envision the restaurant scene with historic Victorian mansions teeming with hot plates of shrimp and grits, and while there are plenty of Southern coastal dishes to go around, the Hostess City of the South offers some cultural experiences you may never have dreamed of, such as stepping into Africa without ever boarding a plane. Imagine authentic African cuisine and decor, including vivid hand-painted art commissioned by natives, where everything is African-sourced, from the masks and crocodiles to the chandeliers fashioned from kudu horns and ostrich eggs.

Located in the iconic Plant Riverside District, Baobab Lounge is named after the majestic baobab tree, Africa's Tree of Life. The menu features a variety of signature beverages and small plates inspired by biltong, a South African–style jerky made in-house of dried, cured meat. In collaboration with the Kessler Collection corporate team, Executive Chef Shahin Afsharian (who is now the chief operating officer at Big Bon Bodega, page 26) designed the menu, explaining how important it was to use vessels that were familiar to make the food

Baobab Lounge features its own wine market. Hand-select bottles from the wine cellar or request a cellar menu from your server. Signature wines from sommelier Tinashe Nyamudoka, a native of Harare, Zimbabwe, and founder of Kumusha Wines, are available. In the Shona language of Zimbabwe, "Kumusha" translates to "your home," "your roots," or "your origin," all of which Nyamudoka used as inspiration for Kumusha wines.

Left: Mr. Richard Kessler designed the space himself with pieces from his personal collection and artwork from different regions throughout Africa. *Center:* The center court of the Power Plant building is full of awe and wonder, including a 135-foot chromed-dipped dinosaur and geodes in brilliant colors. *Right:* Indigenous ingredients and an extensive wine selection make up the uncomplicated and approachable menu. All photos courtesy of Plant Riverside District.

approachable for the right clientele. “Introducing a foreign cuisine to smaller cities is not an easy task,” he says. “Baobab is a clear reflection of bringing vessels to the table that people understand.”

Chef Afsharian, who is part Iranian and part Mexican, incorporated Middle Eastern influences into several of the snacks, showcasing ingredients such as schug, a variety of hot sauce that today is featured in the Bobotie Hand Pies and Lamb Kebabs. While schug may be a foreign concept to some, hand pies and kebabs are the universal language. The menu also has lighter options, such as a cheese board with fruit or an African Dip Duo.

Just outside the main entrance of Baobab Lounge inside the lobby of the Power Plant building, a 135-foot-long chrome-dipped dinosaur hangs from the ceiling alongside geodes, minerals, and fossils dating back millions of years. For chairman and CEO of the Kessler Collection, Richard Kessler, the intention behind Baobab Lounge is to honor the origin of mankind and the world’s natural history. “Mankind was created first out of Africa,” he says. “So, you’ve got minerals and you’ve got mankind. Therefore, we need to honor African history and culture.”

400 W River St.
912-373-9033, plantriverside.com/venues/baobab-lounge

PLANT RIVERSIDE DISTRICT

The destination for entertainment

Designed with families in mind, Plant Riverside District is the center of electric entertainment on Savannah's riverfront, offering 14 varied food and beverage venues, live music, inspired art, carefully curated retail shopping, and luxury accommodations. The 4.5-acre property was the original site of Riverside Station, Savannah's first modern power plant built in 1912. Prior to its most recent transformation, the site was the largest piece of undeveloped National Historic District property in the nation. Enter chairman and CEO of the Kessler Collection, Richard Kessler.

"When I saw the building, I said, I think I can make a hotel out of this building with retail, but it needs to be bigger than that," he says. Richard was born in Savannah and grew up in Rincon, Georgia, earning bachelor's and master's degrees in industrial engineering from Georgia Institute of Technology and later becoming president and CEO of Days Inn at just 29 years old. A nationally recognized hospitality industry leader, Richard founded the Kessler Collection in 1984 as a visionary hospitality brand with 10 culture-rich destinations in Georgia, Florida, Alabama, North and South Carolina, Minnesota, and Colorado.

The planning and construction for Plant Riverside District took nearly 10 years and $375 million, making it the largest redevelopment project in the history of Savannah's Historic Landmark District. "We decided to really create our own concepts instead of franchising concepts, like Baobab Lounge (page 36) and four rooftop lounges," Richard says. "I wanted everything to be unique and particularly designed for Savannah."

The revitalized quarter mile of previously unused riverfront space is now a welcoming family environment, thoughtfully designed so that when you arrive, you never have to leave. Prior to Plant Riverside

Left: Richard Kessler, chairman and CEO of the Kessler Collection, is the visionary behind Plant Riverside District. *Top center:* Enjoy locally brewed beer with a view at the lively Riverside Biergarten situated on the Savannah riverfront. Photo courtesy of Plant Riverside District. *Above center:* Savannah Tequila Co. is a walk-up cantina with a menu of traditional Mexican favorites, such as handmade tacos, flautas, and burritos. Photo courtesy of Plant Riverside District. *Top right:* Stone & Webster Chophouse delivers a new take on an American chophouse experience with a premium selection of wine, prime steaks, and seafood. Photo courtesy of Plant Riverside District. *Above right:* Myrtle & Rose Rooftop Garden features botanical cocktails and breathtaking views. Photo courtesy of Plant Riverside District.

District, Savannah was lacking in options for kids ages 8 to 12 to enjoy. "If you look at the restaurants, kids love pizza and they love Mexican food, so we did the outdoor pavilions, in which they can sit outside and enjoy," says Richard. "The idea behind the pavilions was bringing the seafood and BBQ experience to the riverfront where everybody is. Outdoor, open air. It's really worked well."

Grab a fresh-baked pastry or nutritious smoothie from Turbine Market + Café, or an authentic, Italian-style, house-made gelato at District Gelato. If you're looking for a more upscale fine-dining experience, look no further than Stone & Webster Chophouse, named for the engineers who pioneered Riverside Station. Experience handmade tacos, flautas, and burritos at Savannah Tequila Co. or celebrate Bavarian style with a beer at Riverside Biergarten. Enjoy the view while biting into a tasty smash burger with crispy fries at Riverside Burger. "There's no place you can go in Savannah that has more concentration of entertainment than this," says Richard. "And we're going to keep making it better and better."

400 W River St.
912-373-9100, plantriverside.com

CAREY HILLIARD'S RESTAURANT

Savannah's favorite family restaurant offering seafood and barbecue

During the COVID-19 pandemic, when many restaurants were pivoting to offer curbside service, there was one Savannah restaurant that was light-years ahead of the game. Celebrating more than 63 years in business, Carey Hilliard's has always offered drive-in service at each of its six locations. They're known for fresh seafood and tender barbecue, and everything on the menu is made to order and from scratch.

An excerpt from the restaurant's website reads:

> *After hitch-hiking to Savannah from Jesup, GA, Carey Hilliard opened his first restaurant in 1960, in a closed National Root Beer stand building on Skidaway Rd. and Sunset Drive. Carey and his wife, Kathleen, re-imagined family-priced dining with the convenience of take-out and curbside service. By the 1960s, drive-ups were closing & replaced by a drive-thru, but Carey bucked the trend. He kept the old drive-up we now call the "curb!"*

As it turns out, bucking the trend served Carey well. Although he and his wife tragically passed away in a plane crash in December of 1982, one of their four children, Tim, decided to take on the responsibility of running the family business. At just 23 years old, he became the president and CEO, and the rest is history.

Carey Hilliard's is known for staying open late, serving hand-battered onion rings, fried shrimp, and their famous Brunswick stew from 11 a.m. until midnight, every night. Quick and friendly service, quality food, and family pricing—these are the pillars that have made

Left: Carey Hilliard's has been known for its drive-in, curbside service since the 1960s. *Center:* A photograph recognizing Fred Jordan, an employee for more than 37 years, who is responsible for getting the delivery truck ready and setting up for banquet events. *Right:* The chicken finger platter served with toast and two sides: green beans and french fries.

the restaurant a success and keep customers coming back again and again. Upon a recent visit, Dave M., a Facebook follower, left this friendly comment: "First place I go whenever I come to Savannah!" John W., another Facebook fan, gave the restaurant high praise: "Traveled the world for a living and there is no place like it."

One of the most unique things about Carey Hilliard's is its commitment to its team. They have an employee-recognition program honoring years of service from 10 to 45 years. There are $1,000 bonuses for employees reaching 10 years of service, and at 45 years of service, the employee gets to choose a $15,000 cash reward or car worth $45,000. Visit any location and you will see large black-and-white canvas photos of long-standing employees adorning the walls. Carey Hilliard's staff is a family of its own; the waitstaff, cooks, and management are the backbone of the business and are treated as such. Lifetime careers are a family tradition here.

Multiple locations
Flagship: 3316 Skidaway Rd.
912-354-7240, careyhilliards.com

"There's always something special cookin' at Carey Hilliard's!" If you're on a budget, save money by looking for the monthly specials, such as the deviled crab or the fried tail-on white shrimp.

BARNES RESTAURANT

Pit-cooked barbecue since 1975

Barnes Restaurant is the kind of place that is one with its community, where everyone who is in the know goes anytime they want good home cooking, and especially after church on Sunday. You can smell the famous pit-cooked barbecue from the time you drive up in the parking area and your mouth starts watering for those quintessential classic Southern side dishes, like red rice, collard greens, and potato salad. It's one of Savannah's landmark restaurants that embodies the qualities of familiarity, consistency, and home.

A native of Savannah, the late Nesbert "Bo" Barnes was born in 1928. Some of his early memories were of the Great Depression, when pork sold for a quarter a pound, his son Alan says. Nesbert would later serve in the Korean War, returning home to become a foreman of the composing room at the *Savannah Morning News*, where he worked for 22 years.

In the mid-1970s, after purchasing a Dairy Queen and operating it for a few years, Nesbert wanted a place of his own. He purchased a Carey Hillard's take-out location on Waters Avenue in Savannah near 68th Street and named it Barnes Restaurant. He would spend nearly 20 years in that location before he and his son, Hugh, expanded the restaurant and menu in a new location next door with the purchase of additional land.

Today, Barnes Restaurant remains in that same location and has been serving rotisserie chicken, seafood, ribs, sandwiches, salads, and barbecue the same way every day since 1975.

Barnes has been catering for nearly five decades with a great-tasting menu that won't break the bank. From events for 50 to 5,000, they offer full-service catering or pickup options.

Top left: Images of iconic Savannah decorate the interior, depicting the James Oglethorpe Monument in Chippewa Square and the Forsyth Park fountain. *Above left:* Hamburger steak with a baked potato. *Top right:* Pulled pork with Barnes's famous barbecue sauce, green beans, french fries, and toast. *Above right:* With its wooden shiplap and exposed brick walls, Barnes Restaurant exudes warmth and charm.

In addition to consistency, Barnes's barbecue is popular because they use only the freshest, highest-quality Boston butts and premium barbecue-style ribs. In the South you can't serve barbecue without a good sauce, and Barnes has you covered with their signature recipe, which is bottled and shipped all over the world. Made in-house from scratch, the sauce is a family tradition that is balanced and versatile. It draws on regional inspiration with a well-rounded base of mustard and ketchup. Try it on a sandwich, pulled or chopped pork, ribs, or just about anything on the menu. Also, don't miss the daily specials, where you can order oxtails with white rice and corn bread or homemade meatloaf with two sides and toast.

When you visit Barnes, you'll notice a sign on the exterior pointing left for to-go and right for dine in. No matter which option you choose, you'll be glad you did.

5320 Waters Ave.
912-354-8745, barnesrestaurant.com

BYRD'S FAMOUS COOKIES

Baking history since 1924

Cookies bring a smile to everyone's face, and in Savannah there's one cookie company that's been a part of the city's fabric since 1924. Today, Byrd Cookie Company is one of the largest and fastest-growing independent cookie, snack, and gift companies in the US, with retail stores in Georgia, South Carolina, and Tennessee. But it all started with one flavor—the Scotch Oatmeal Cookie—in a small downtown bakery near City Market, one of Savannah's best-known gathering places.

Benjamin Tillman "Pop" Byrd Sr. sold his famous Scotch oatmeal cookies out of large glass jars, at two for a penny, to stores around town in his Model T Ford. They became very popular among the locals, and no other bakery item was as unique. This special cookie remains a part of the lineup today, freshly baked from a family recipe that has been passed down through the generations. The Scotch oatmeal cookie—the OG—combines oats, cinnamon, vanilla, and raisin paste to create a delicious, crunchy, one-of-a-kind cookie that customers have loved for 100 years.

With 16 sweet and salty cookie flavors to choose from, you can try before you buy. Each Byrd Cookie shop is known for its sample bar, where you can taste inspired sweet flavors like Key Lime Coolers, Cupcake Cookies, and Benne Wafers, or savory selections such as Jalapeño Cheddar Biscuits, Cheddar Pecan Biscuits, and Everything Cheddar Biscuits (inspired by everything bagel seasoning). The small, round, bite-size cookies are distinct in their shape and style, and for a personal touch, each bakery bag is filled by hand. New cookie flavors and products are always being introduced, such as fun, hand-decorated rice crispy treats.

CEO Stephanie Curl Lindley is a fourth-generation owner and has been instrumental in expanding the family-owned business to

Left: Employees stand ready with a smile to serve you at the sample bar. *Right:* You can fill your own cookie jar with any flavor you choose.

include strategic partnerships with major retailers such as L.L.Bean, Bergdorf Goodman, United Airlines, and Delta. The company also creates private-label items for Neiman Marcus, Ritz-Carlton, and Cumberland Farms. Under Stephanie's leadership in 2017, the company announced a $4 million expansion at its bakery in Savannah, adding 10,000 square feet of space, significantly increasing production capacity, and creating more than 50 new jobs. The following summer, Byrd Cookie Company installed a new 170-foot oven, allowing for the production of more than one billion cookies each year—and the operation continues to grow.

When you visit Savannah, don't leave without one of Byrd's signature cookie tins specially designed with iconic cityscapes such as River Street and the Forsyth Park fountain.

6700 Waters Ave.
912-355-1716

423 E River St.
912-721-1566

213 W Julian St.
912-721-1563

9 Mill Creek Cir. A–2, Pooler
912-721-1560

www.byrdcookiecompany.com

Byrd's Key Lime Coolers made history in 1990 when they became the first cookie to win "Dessert of the Year" at the Specialty Food Association's Fancy Food Show.

LEOPOLD'S ICE CREAM

"Good Things to Eat! Good Things to Drink!"

During the summertime in Savannah, there's one place that everyone goes to cool down and chill out, and that's world-famous Leopold's Ice Cream. Since 1919, generations of Savannahians and tourists from far and wide have enjoyed the handcrafted ice cream, soda-fountain milkshakes, and banana splits made from the original, secret recipes handed down to Stratton Leopold by his father.

Leopold's Ice Cream was founded by three brothers from Greece: George, Peter, and Basil, who learned the art of candy and dessert making from an uncle who had previously settled in America. Peter's son, Stratton, would carry on the family legacy upon his father's passing. Stratton learned how to create premium ice cream as a young boy, and he spent many days as a kid behind the soda fountain, scooping ice cream, and washing dishes. The first ice cream parlor was located on the corner of Gwinnett and Habersham Streets, but many years later, in 2004, Leopold's Ice Cream would open a flagship store on Broughton Street, one of the city's most prominent streets full of shops and restaurants.

Today that retro ice cream parlor contains memorabilia from its first location, including the black marble soda fountain, the wooden back bar, and the telephone booth.

Leopold's Ice Cream has more than 23 inventive ice cream flavors made one batch at a time, including singer and songwriter Johnny

Get there early or prepare to wait in line. Leopold's Ice Cream was named one of the Top 10 Ice Cream Parlors in the World by the *Toronto Sun* and can be shipped nationwide, directly to your door!

Left: Inside the ice cream shop, owner Stratton Leopold smiles proudly in front of his movie posters. *Center:* A rainbow of colorful ice cream flavors atop a waffle cone. *Right:* A huckleberry fruit sundae with two scoops of vanilla ice cream, whipped cream, and pecans. All photos courtesy of Leopold's Ice Cream.

Mercer's favorite, Tutti Frutti, featuring rum ice cream, candied fruit, and fresh-roasted Georgia pecans. Here's the scoop: Johnny grew up a block away from Leopold's and worked at the shop as a boy. Try the classic Peanut Butter Chippy with all-natural peanut butter ice cream and milk chocolate chips, or the Honey Almond & Cream made with Savannah Bee Company honey. The soda fountain and café menu also includes brownie and hot fudge sundaes; specialty hot beverages; and homemade freshly baked pastries such as cakes, pies, cupcakes, and cookies.

One of the most unique things about this Savannah tradition may be its nod to Hollywood and the movies. Movie posters and photographs of notable actors and actresses fill the walls, and that's because in addition to being the owner and operator of Leopold's Ice Cream, Stratton is a blockbuster movie producer. He produced *Mission Impossible III* and *The General's Daughter* to name a few.

Join celebrities such as Sylvester Stallone and Tom Cruise—and even presidents—who've tasted Leopold's Ice Cream and experience this memorable frozen delight for yourself.

212 E Broughton St.
912-234-4442, leopoldsIcecream.com

You can also find Leopold's at two spots in Savannah/Hilton Head International Airport
400 Airways Ave.
912-483-0122

COTTON & RYE

Refined Southern cooking with Jewish influence

Zach Shultz, owner of Cotton & Rye, spent his childhood summers in Palm Beach, Florida, with an older cousin, a talented chef who owned several high-end Italian restaurants. "Growing up, I would stay with him over the summers, and I would just tag along and work with him at all of his restaurants." From an early age, he was attracted to the restaurant industry, hungry for his own success. He grew up in Savannah and would later graduate from the culinary arts program at Johnson & Wales University in Miami, eventually returning home to make his own mark in the Hostess City of the South.

Throughout middle and high school, Zach worked in back-of-house positions as a dishwasher, busboy, and expeditor, anything that would work with his school schedule. It wasn't until 2003, when his dad took a job in Tampa, that he began gaining experience in high-volume restaurants and scratch kitchens. "My last year of culinary school, I went and worked under a chef whose name could carry me outside of the city."

That chef was Allen Susser, a James Beard Foundation "Best Chefs in America" winner. With that training as a part of his culinary chops, Zach made his way down to Key West. There he worked at Louie's Backyard, a fine-dining restaurant with an ocean view, where notable chefs such as Norman Van Aken and Charlie Trotter got started. These experiences and his Jewish heritage would shape Zach's vision for his first restaurant concept.

"Coming back to Savannah, I always wanted to open a Southern restaurant, but I wanted it to have modern technique infused with Southern cuisine," he says. He opened Cotton & Rye in the summer of 2015, after renovating a building that had earlier been used by a

Left: Cocoa-nut macaroon layer cake with cashew coconut brittle and frozen blonde chocolate custard by in-house pastry chef Peanut Ayers. *Center:* Award-winning crispy chicken wings made with spicy honey, sumac, chipotle morita, and a cheeseburger topped with a fried green tomato, american cheese, peppercorn mayo, served with french fries. *Right:* Owner Zach Shultz (left) and Executive Chef Caleb Ayers in front of "Hot Rye," the restaurant's food truck. All photos courtesy of Cotton & Rye.

bank. In the name, Cotton refers to the Southern influence in the menu, while Rye nods to the heavy bourbon bar.

At Cotton & Rye, everything is made to order in-house, including charcuterie, fresh bread, and desserts. They even grind their own meat and smoke bacon behind the building. "We don't buy anything premade," Zach says. Though the restaurant is refined in its French style of service, you'll find burgers, chicken wings, and fried chicken on its approachable menu. Expect hearty portions and bold flavor profiles, such as buttermilk rye corn bread with rosemary and burnt honey. All ingredients are sourced from small, local farms. "The ingredients we use are the best you can get," he says. "We take a lot of pride in where our ingredients come from."

1801 Habersham St.
912-777-6286, cottonandrye.com

Hot Rye—"Fire Food on Wheels"—is a sandwich-based food truck allowing guests to experience lunch service outdoors, since the restaurant is only open for dinner. Try the Loaded Latkes featuring flavors such as Nashville hot, chili cheese, or sour cream and caramelized onion latkes!

AUSPICIOUS BAKING Co

Handcrafted breads and pastries

Kaytlin (Katie) Bryant and Mark Ekstrom, owners of Auspicious Baking Co., left the Pocono Mountains of Pennsylvania to bring a little taste of the North to Savannah. The community came out in droves to support this couple's American dream, and they never imagined it would take off like a rocket. Fast-forward to present day—they continue baking fresh loaves and croissants, flaky pop-tarts, and warm cinnamon buns from scratch, and selling out faster than they can preheat the oven.

The couple met through a mutual friend. Both had worked in the restaurant business for several years. Mark spent his days at a little Greek deli, later working for a large chain restaurant, and Katie spent many years working in the back- and front-of-house for a historic fine-dining establishment. "We decided we wanted to leave the Poconos to see what else was out there. We packed up everything we had in a van and we left the Poconos with no plans," says Mark. They road-tripped down the East Coast, stumbled upon Savannah, and fell in love with the city. The adventure continued to Florida, but they didn't stay long. "After a couple of days, we both looked at each other and said, 'Savannah is where we want to go,'" Mark says. "So, we turned around, came back up, and within three days, we both had

The European-style bakery case is filled with carb-loaded items and savory selections, including chocolate and ham-and-cheese croissants, soft pretzels, and cheesesteak quiche. You can also enjoy cold-case options, such as hummus, baba ghanoush, and soup. Every menu item has a thoughtful connection to family ties and nostalgia.

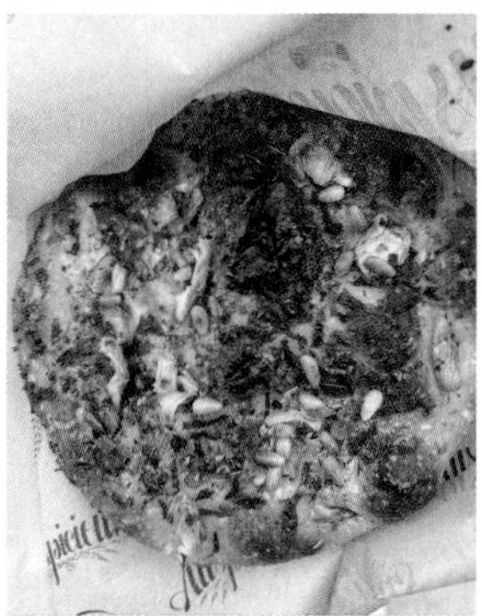

Left: Coconut cream pie shines brightly in the center of this Sunday spread, surrounded by cookies, cinnamon rolls, and Danishes. Photo courtesy of Auspicious Baking Co. *Center left:* Focaccia featuring pine nuts, artichoke hearts, lemon, and basil. Photo courtesy of Auspicious Baking Co. *Center right:* A Sunday bake assortment of handcrafted breads and pastries. Photo courtesy of Auspicious Baking Co. *Right:* Katie Bryant and Mark Ekstrom, owners of Auspicious Baking Co.

a job and an apartment in Savannah. We literally scraped the change out of our cupholders to get our electric deposit in."

When Katie was just 11 years old, her father, who was a chef, passed away. With the help of his life insurance policy, Katie and Mark were able to purchase their first convection oven and opened Auspicious Baking Co. in 2017 on Father's Day weekend to honor him. "It was very serendipitous," Katie says. "We just felt like, even 10 years after his passing, he's still teaching and helping me, and aiding in my progress." Mark and Katie made a name for themselves in that first location for about three years, until they outgrew it. As fate would have it, a Great Harvest Bread Company was simultaneously closing just seven miles down the road, and the couple seized the opportunity to move there. More than six years and 30 employees later, business is still booming. "We knew without the support of our community that our business wouldn't be successful," says Katie. "As we've grown our business, we've grown our family. It's been very welcoming for us."

The word *auspicious* means "conducive to success," a name never more fitting than for the bakery.

7360 Skidaway Rd.
912-349-3444, auspiciousbakingco.com

CLARY'S CAFE

Traditional diner favorites made right

Pass by Clary's Cafe on any given weekend in Savannah, and you'll see the outdoor tables full of guests sipping coffee or cold iced tea under the shade of the striped awning, dogs on leashes next to their owners, silver bowls of water nearby. Evolved from a drugstore with a lunch counter and soda fountain in 1903, Clary's Cafe rose to fame after its appearance in John Berendt's 1994 novel, *Midnight in the Garden of Good and Evil*, and Clint Eastwood's 1997 movie adaptation.

Berendt called Clary's Cafe "a clearinghouse of information, a bourse of gossip," where the cast exchanged ideas and got acquainted. In a 2014 article titled "The Best Breakfast Joints in the South," *Garden & Gun* magazine's John Kessler referred to the café as "a hash house in the most exalted sense of the term."

On the corner of Jones and Abercorn Streets, the pet-friendly café is known as "Savannah's Breakfast Restaurant," offering traditional diner favorites made right every day of the week. They serve breakfast all day, with house specialties that include freshly homemade corned beef hash, which starts with kosher corned beef briskets in the kitchen and is served piled high on a plate with eggs of any style and buttermilk biscuits. For those with a sweet tooth, the Malted Waffle Supreme is crisp, dusted with powdered sugar, and topped with your choice of strawberries or blueberries and a big dollop of whipped cream. Peanut butter lovers should try "The Elvis," thick-sliced bread

Clary's Cafe offers free Wi-Fi, and there are discounts for members of the military, Savannah College of Art and Design affiliates, and the Girl Scouts of the USA.

Top left: The friendly faces of the Clary's Cafe team. *Above left:* Clary's Cafe website says of the jumbo homemade éclair, "Sinful, but you must try one!" *Top right:* Freshly homemade corned beef hash served with two eggs, breakfast potatoes, and a biscuit. *Above right:* Dogs are welcome to dine outdoors, where they receive free treats and water. All photos courtesy of Clary's Cafe.

stuffed with peanut butter and bananas. The menu features satisfying and hearty portions for breakfast and lunch, with a tempting display case of scratch-made desserts and pastries. Famous for their jumbo homemade éclair filled with bavarian creme custard and topped with rich dark chocolate, it can feed two or more, or just one if you're feeling a bit adventurous.

The interior dining room is filled with large, round tables for bigger parties and smaller, two- and four-top tables with green granite. Local art and memorabilia fill the wood-paneled and exposed-brick walls, including stained glass windows. One busy black-and-white photograph of happy, well-dressed patrons and their children enjoying cold ice cream cones is labeled "Sunday after church at Clary's in 1952." Black-and-white checkerboard flooring contributes to the eclectic vibe of the diner, known for its friendly service and approachable food.

If that lunch counter could talk, it could tell some stories.

404 Abercorn St.
912-233-0402, claryscafe.com

GEORGIA QUEEN

Cruise, dance, and dine

The port city of Savannah may not have a cruise ship terminal, but that doesn't mean you won't have an opportunity to see the city from the unique vantage point of the waterfront. Docked daily next to the exact location where General James Oglethorpe landed in Georgia's first city is the bright red and white *Georgia Queen*, a center-stage fixture on River Street and the largest and grandest riverboat of its kind in the US. Offering a variety of sightseeing excursions from narrated harbor cruises to Sunday brunch, dinner entertainment, and Monday gospel dinner cruises, the *Georgia Queen* is part of the Savannah Riverboat Cruises fleet established in 1991 by Capt. Jonathan H. Claughton.

Originally built for $14 million in 1995 as a luxury floating casino on the Mississippi River, the *Georgia Queen* is an 1800s paddlewheel-style riverboat measuring 230 feet long, 64 foot wide, and 68 feet tall, encompassing an impressive 38,000 total square feet. Capt. Claughton introduced the ship to Savannah in 2016, after making the journey 2,800 miles down the Mississippi River, across the Gulf of Mexico, and down and around the shorelines of Florida and Key West.

With a capacity for 1,000 passengers and 200 crew members, the vessel is the size of a small cruise ship. It features three grand ballrooms with over 15,000 square feet of dining space, a sprawling 5,000-square-foot, fully open-air top deck with patio seating, and a multi-deck, fully equipped gourmet kitchen. Menus vary depending on the tour you choose. On the Sunday brunch cruise, indulge in Southern favorites such as fried chicken and shrimp and grits. The dinner entertainment cruise includes a specially prepared buffet-style dinner complete with a beef carving station; the fresh catch of the day; and seasonal sides such as squash casserole, potatoes au gratin, and fresh garden greens. Each experience allows you to

Left: If you are celebrating an anniversary, birthday, or special occasion, special events packages are offered with charming details such as balloons, roses, and cake. *Top center:* Author Rebekah Faulk Lingenfelser at Eastern Wharf, as the *Georgia Queen* cruises up the Savannah River. Photo courtesy of Sarah Peacock. *Above center:* Inside the *Georgia Queen*, grand chandeliers, comfortable seating, and draped windows create an inviting atmosphere. A specially prepared buffet awaits, accompanied by a full bar. *Right:* Author Rebekah Faulk Lingenfelser and her husband, Kurt, celebrate a wedding anniversary aboard the bow of the *Georgia Queen*, with views of the Talmadge Memorial Bridge in the background.

indulge in local, Southern cuisine as you savor relaxing views, scenic photo opportunities, and refreshing river breezes.

The riverboat tours head upriver into the port of Savannah, then turn around and head back under the Eugene Talmadge Memorial Bridge past the historic riverfront. The tours continue downriver, passing the world famous *Waving Girl, Florence Martus*, through the shipyards, and just past the tip of Hutchinson Island and Old Fort Jackson.

If you're looking for an adventure, look no further than Savannah Riverboat Cruises, a one-of-a-kind attraction in Georgia's historic waterfront city.

9 E River St.
912-232-6404, savannahriverboat.com

Savannah Riverboat Cruises boasts the Hostess City's only riverboat tours and dining experience. Be sure to check out the *Georgia Queen*'s sister ship, the *Savannah River Queen*.

THE OLDE PINK HOUSE RESTAURANT & TAVERN

More than 250 years of history

Originally built in 1771, The Olde Pink House Restaurant & Tavern is one of Savannah's most exquisite fine-dining destinations, offering classic Southern cuisine in a stately Georgia mansion. Nestled in the Historic Landmark District on a brick-paved street facing Reynolds Square, the home itself, with its pink exterior, is as much of a draw for locals and tourists as the food itself.

Built by native Savannahian and American merchant James Habersham Jr., the original home, known as the Habersham House, had just five rooms. The basement housed the kitchen and laundry rooms but today has been reimagined as Planter's Tavern, a dark, moody pub where the locals often slip in for a signature cocktail. It is rumored that the ghost of Habersham still visits. General manager of The Olde Pink House, Craig Jeffress, says the restaurant's unmistakable pink color came from Habersham's desire to make his wife happy. She appealed to her husband that all the wealthy people in town had stucco covering their homes and asked him to do the same. "So, as a good husband, he covered his home in stucco," Craig told *The Dish* on CBS *Saturday Morning*. "What they didn't understand is that everything in South Georgia sweats in the summertime, including the red clay bricks. So, their gorgeous stucco home turned pink, over and over and over again." Now that distinction is a part of the home's character and story, forever ingrained in its walls.

The restaurant includes 13 unique dining spaces for guests to enjoy. From the grand ballroom to the master bedroom, every inch of The Olde Pink House offers a dining experience and color all its own.

Top left: The Olde Pink House Restaurant & Tavern is one of kind in Savannah's culinary landscape. *Above left:* Expansive murals featuring hand-painted wallpaper fill the grand ballroom. *Top right:* Crispy scored flounder with apricot shallot sauce is a 30-year-old dish at The Olde Pink House, served with creamy stone-ground grits and collard greens. Photo courtesy of The Olde Pink House Restaurant & Tavern. *Above right:* The famous Praline Basket is filled with vanilla ice cream and topped with berries for a satisfying end to the meal. Photo courtesy of The Olde Pink House Restaurant & Tavern.

Throughout the mansion, crystal chandeliers, hand-painted wallpaper, fireplaces, and revived period pieces selected by owner Donna Moeckel create an elegant ambiance that embodies Southern charm and hospitality. When you walk into the landmark today, you will pass through the original front door.

The cuisine is sourced from the waters just off Savannah's coast. "On the menu, we strive to represent this region incredibly well," says Craig. Their signature dish—crispy scored flounder with a chocolate apricot shallot sauce—has been on the menu for more than 30 years, and for good reason. The praline basket is popular for dessert, and when it comes to drinks, their signature spirits are exclusive to the Olde Pink House. They partner with distilleries around the country to blend their own custom offerings.

"It's very humbling when people stand in line for what you do," says Craig. "We never want to take that for granted."

23 Abercorn St.
912-232-4286, theoldepinkhouserestaurant.com

TEQUILA'S TOWN MEXICAN RESTAURANT

Authentic cuisine and world-class tequila

Sergio Calderon, Sergio Ortiz, and Temo Ortiz are the three business partners behind Tequila's Town Mexican Restaurant. Consistently voted "Best Mexican Restaurant and Tequila Bar in Savannah" by local media, they succeed at their mission to serve fresh, authentic Mexican cuisine and to offer the best tequila selection in town.

The leadership team, made up of two brothers and a compadre, has more than 50 years of combined food-industry experience. United by their love for food and people and by their high standards for excellence in service, the family-owned-and-operated business is a Taco Tuesday favorite and the only place to be on Cinco de Mayo in Savannah. With roots in Morelia, Michoacán, a bustling city in central Mexico, the managing partners are longtime Savannah residents who treat each customer like family. When they were planning the business, the partners envisioned a casual yet modern Mexican eatery that would become the place to have great tequila and tacos. Hence, the name "Tequila's Town" was born.

Sergio's Carnitas de Michoacán

Now you can make Tequila's Town's most celebrated regional dish at home, courtesy of Sergio Ortiz, executive chef and partner. Fill delicious tacos or tortas (sandwiches) with the melt-in-your-mouth meat.

In 2020, Tequila's Town expanded to offer Tacos + Tequila in midtown Savannah, an authentic outdoor taqueria and tequila bar dishing 18 different street tacos, Mexican antojitos, small bites, and more than 80 artisanal and small-batch spirits.

Left: The Carnitas Michoacán are made with tender, beer-marinated pork chunks seasoned and fried to perfection. *Right:* Business partners Sergio Calderon, Temo Ortiz, and Sergio Ortiz (left to right). All photos courtesy of Tequila's Town.

Ingredients

- 4 lbs. fatty pork shoulder, cut into 3-inch chunks
- 1½ c. water
- 1 can of beer
- 1 orange, cut in half
- ½ lemon
- ¼ c. pork lard or vegetable oil (dietary preference)
- 7 garlic cloves, peeled
- 2 Tb. of sugar (brown sugar gives this dish a kick!)
- 2 tsp. fine salt, or 4 tsp. kosher salt

Preparation

Put all the ingredients in a wide, six- to-seven-quart heavy pot (don't worry if the pork is not completely covered) and bring the water to a boil. Lower the heat and simmer, stirring only as needed, until the pork chunks are fork-tender and the liquid has completely evaporated. This could take one and a half to two hours. Discard the orange and lemon pieces. If the liquid hasn't evaporated after two hours, transfer the pork pieces to a bowl and let the liquid continue to bubble away, stirring often, until it has evaporated completely. Preheat the oven to 450 degrees Fahrenheit. Transfer the pork and fat to an ovenproof dish, if necessary, and brown the pork, uncovered in the oven for 30 minutes.

Tequila's Town

109 Whitaker St.
912-236-3222

7360 Skidaway Rd.
912-226-3307
tequilastown.com

13475 Atlantic Blvd., Ste.1
Jacksonville, FL
904-513-4194

Tacos + Tequila

1611 Habersham St.
912-303-5454

405 Pooler Pkwy., Ste. 2, Pooler
912-737-2134

tacosplustequila.com

McDONOUGH'S RESTAURANT & LOUNGE

Karaoke, Irish pub fare, and shenanigans

Every community needs that quintessential neighborhood bar, the go-to hangout spot for good times with the best of friends you have yet to meet. For nearly 40 years, that place has been McDonough's Restaurant & Lounge, famous for its fun karaoke stage and late-night Irish-inspired pub fare. Your Savannah experience is not complete until you've had a strong drink at the friendly bar or crooned your cares away on center stage, where celebrities like Ben Affleck, Stan Lee, and even Clint Eastwood have been known to hold the mic.

The late Savannah legend William "Billy" Lee opened McDonough's Restaurant & Lounge at the corner of McDonough and Drayton Streets on St. Patrick's Day in 1987. Introducing Savannah to his restaurant on March 17 was foreshadowing: McDonough's remains the yearly headquarters for the St. Patrick's Day festival, opening at 7 a.m. with its legendary traditional Irish breakfast buffet. With its prime location near the parade route, the restaurant is a popular spot to grab a to-go drink.

Billy grew up in Savannah, playing basketball at Armstrong Junior College, today known as Georgia Southern University–Armstrong Campus, and later joined the US Army, serving in the Korean War. He returned to Savannah and would own several restaurants before opening McDonough's Restaurant & Lounge and, in the early 2000s, Billy's

McDonough's Inn is conveniently located above the restaurant and lounge, with two comfortable units available for renting.

Left: Many a good night has started or ended at this convivial corner bar. *Center:* McDonough's Restaurant & Lounge offers hearty bar food, such as these chicken wings, which come in a variety of flavors from buffalo to kickin' bourbon. *Right:* McDonough's is *the* spot for karaoke in Savannah. All photos courtesy of McDonough's Restaurant Lounge.

Place, located on the second floor of the same building. The likable, good-natured atmosphere at Savannah's signature Irish pub is credited to Billy's big heart for people and the kindness he showed to all who knew him. Today, the business is run by three of his children, who carry on his legacy: Deborah, Joseph, and Mike.

Year-round, McDonough's is open daily with a kitchen that doesn't close until the wee hours of the morning. Serving breakfast, lunch, and dinner, their offerings include pub classics such as shepherd's pie and deep-fried Irish egg rolls made with corned beef, sauerkraut, and swiss cheese. Try Billy's helluva steak or the Farmhouse burger with bacon, gouda, avocado, a fried egg, and bacon jam. To quench your thirst, McDonough's has a full-service bar featuring draft Georgia beer, plus one of the longest happy hours in the city.

Whether you're a sports fan, a service industry employee, part of a wedding after-party, or a singer looking for your next big break, make plans to indulge in shenanigans and dance the night away at this party pad, an integral part of Savannah's nightlife.

21 E McDonough St.
912-233-6136, mcdonoughslounge.com

BELFORD'S SAVANNAH SEAFOOD AND STEAKS

USDA steaks, crab cakes, and fine wines

Inside of Belford's Savannah Seafood and Steaks, exposed brick walls and copper pipe create an industrial-chic, sophisticated ambiance complemented by white tablecloths and black-and-white framed photographs of days gone by. The restaurant, known for its USDA Prime steaks, crab cakes, and fine wines, anchors the corner of City Market, which once served as the bustling and commercial heart of early Savannah.

The sizable brick building was originally constructed in 1902 for the Savannah Hebrew Congregation to be used as office space for a synagogue. "The backstory to that is, all through the 1700s and 1800s, the Jewish population were the money managers for the cotton and slave owners, so there's a deep history here," says Andy Gromet, general manager of Belford's Savannah, an employee for 11 years. The two-story structure was sold in 1923 to W.T. Belford for $23,000. The Belford family turned the building into Belford's Wholesale Food Company, which served as a grocery store until the 1970s. "They used to kill pigs and chickens in the basement here, and sell groceries and produce," says Andy. "The streets here were all lined with vendors." On the front and sides of the restaurant today, remnants of the original signage can still be seen through the paint on the red brick building.

Belford's Savannah offers a pet-friendly covered patio, perfect for people watching and taking in all that the National Landmark Historic District has to offer.

Left: The lobster gnocchi is the chef's favorite dish featuring an eight-ounce lobster tail, house-made gnocchi, asparagus, heirloom tomatoes, lobster cream, and parmesan. Photo courtesy of Belford's Savannah. *Top center:* A 40-day, wet-aged USDA Prime bone-in 18-ounce rib eye steak, grilled asparagus, and fried potatoes. Photo courtesy of Belford's Savannah. *Above center:* Belford's award-winning jumbo lump crab cake with spiced tomato jam and charred poblano lime aioli. Photo courtesy of Belford's Savannah. *Center right:* Executive Chef "Bobby J." with a platter of fried green tomatoes and spicy rémoulade. *Right:* Belford's Savannah anchors the corner of City Market, directly across from Vinnie Van GoGo's.

For more than 27 years, Belford's Savannah has made a name for itself as an award-winning restaurant, consistently ranked among the city's best destinations to dine. On Saturdays and Sundays the champagne brunch is a must-try for the bottomless mimosas and bellinis as well as the fresh-baked basket of biscuits served with orange wild berry jam and local Savannah honey butter. The menu, made from scratch daily, features main dishes such as shrimp, greens and grits, oven-roasted local trout, and crab Benedict.

"We're all about three things that make our restaurant successful, and that's great food, great service, and a clean bathroom," says Andy.

Executive Chef Jason Day, known as Bobby J., has been with Belford's for more than six years and says it's the family atmosphere that has kept him there. Because Belford's is located in one of the South's most popular travel destinations, a lot of the guests who come through the doors of Belford's are out-of-town visitors, but one thing is certain: everyone is treated like family.

"You're welcome; we want you to be happy; we want you coming back," says Andy.

315 W Saint Julian St.
912-233-2626, belfordssavannah.com

THE LITTLE CROWN BY PIE SOCIETY

Georgia's smallest pie house and pub

Take a drive through Savannah's City Market, and you can't miss the brightly painted blue corner building on the endcap of Jefferson Street. There, you'll find the Little Crown by Pie Society, Georgia's smallest British pie house and pub serving authentic British food, a full bar with craft cocktails, and a small slice of the UK.

Inside, a cozy interior boasts just eight bar seats and two small dining rooms down the corridor in the back of the restaurant. The Little Crown is owned by "Mum Gill" and her three adult children, Melissa, Emma, and Edward (Ed), from Staffordshire, England. Gill, Melissa, and Ed moved to Savannah in 2013 to join Emma, who was already living stateside, to open the business. Their first location was in neighboring Pooler, Georgia, and after much success they welcomed the opportunity to open a second location the following year. "Our recipes are traditional to Staffordshire, England, where we are from, and we bake everything from scratch early in the mornings," says Melissa Wagstaff, co-owner. On the menu, choose from savory pies, like the Steak & Ale Pie, a double-crusted meat pie with slow-cooked steak and onions in a rich gravy made with British beer. You can also opt for quiches, pork pies, and hot pastries and rolls, such as the Savannah-famous sausage rolls. Uncommon desserts tempt the taste buds: try the cherry shortbread; Victoria sponge cake; or banoffee pie, a combination of bananas, toffee, and cream pie.

"We wanted to revolutionize British food in America," says Melissa. "It really doesn't have a great reputation and is often thought of as bland and flavorless. We wanted to change that by combining

Top left: The bright blue paint and gold lettering make this restaurant a standout in City Market. *Above left:* The "Strawberry Fields Forever" cocktail made with fresh strawberry puree, gin, and St. Germaine. *Center:* Melissa Wagstaff and her brother Edward Wagstaff, co-owners. *Top right:* Steak & Ale pie and a pint of Boddingtons. *Above right:* Dine inside "The Snug," an intimate seating area in the back of the restaurant. All photos courtesy of Linda Rowe.

our older authentic recipes with new, more modern flavors from across the UK and other parts of the world." Melissa's brother Ed is the head baker and chef. From the age of 14 he trained in a bakery in England, later becoming a butcher and fishmonger, and uses a lot of those skills in his scratch-made cooking today.

Perfect for grabbing on the go for a stroll through City Market, the pies pair well with Savannah's open container policy. Harry Potter fans, rejoice! Butterbeer is the most popular cocktail. "We have an ever-changing menu of British-themed house cocktails," says Melissa. "The drinks have a big gin focus, and we make a lot of our syrups in-house using fresh ingredients."

It's a great spot to make new friends; the space may be intimate, but it boasts big flavors.

The Little Crown by Pie Society
19 Jefferson St.
912-238-1144

Pie Society
1215 E US Hwy. 80, Ste. 200, Pooler
912-348-2318

thebritishpiecompany.com

Pie Society also operates "Blue Betty," a food truck that can be booked for catering and events.

STARLAND YARD

A food truck park

Shipping containers stacked tall and painted in bright colors define the perimeter around Savannah's only food truck park, Starland Yard, located at the corner of 40th Street and Desoto Avenue in the eclectic and artistic community known as Starland District. The good-time destination opened in 2019 with one idea in mind: to be an outdoor community space where everyone could come to enjoy a variety of good food and drink alfresco.

"We wanted to be a space that is family friendly, a bar and a community space," says Ava Pandiani, general manager of Starland Yard. "Savannah is so beautiful, and we saw that there just weren't many fully outdoor places to enjoy eating and drinking outside. Plus, you can bring your dog, which is maybe the best feature of all."

The Yard, as it is often called by the locals, is complete with cornhole boards, outdoor games, and picnic tables with umbrellas. Permanent structures anchoring the space are the Yard Bar and Chef Kyle Jacovino's Vittoria Pizzeria Napoletana, with more to come. Over 16 food trucks are on a rotating schedule, with one to four on-site daily, keeping the selection of delicious fare fresh.

The Yard Bar offers local draft beer from Georgia breweries like Two Tides (Savannah) and Creature Comforts (Athens), wine, cocktails, and frozen drinks. The brick-and-mortar pizzeria features naturally leavened Neapolitan pies, such as the Classic Margherita or La Diavola

The truck schedule, available on the website, lets you know which food trucks are on-site daily. Guest parking is available in the lot behind the Yard next to Two Tides Brewery (entrance on 41st Street), and in the lot across the street on Whitaker and 40th Streets.

Top left: Live music adds a fun vibe to the lively crowd. *Above left:* Starland Yard offers something for everyone with plenty of options to choose from. *Top center:* The Crudo is a white pie with whipped ricotta, arugula, Sicilian olive oil, and your choice of salumi. *Above center:* Food trucks featuring a variety of cuisine from Cuban and Jamaican to British and bayou can be found on-site seven days a week. *Right:* Starland Yard is constructed of shipping containers, a gesture to the Port of Savannah, which as of 2021, was the third-busiest seaport in the US. All photos courtesy of Starland Yard.

with calabrese sausage, soppressata, Calabrian chilies, marinara, and mozzarella. Sandwiches, salads, and sweets are also on the menu. Chef Jacovino trained in Italy for six months, where he completed an apprenticeship with a Venetian pizzaiolo and learned the pasta-making techniques of Puglia. Today, he shares his deep appreciation for the slow food movement and Italian cuisine with a baker's approach to pizza, regional Southern influences, and local ingredients.

One of the unique things about Starland Yard is the method of payment. When you arrive, you'll visit the check-in booth to swipe your card and set up a tab. All purchases during your time at the Yard will be added to your tab accordingly, and when you're ready to leave, simply visit the checkout window to close out. Starland Yard curates special events, featuring live music, art, and culture weekly. It's the perfect place to visit if you're with a group who may not agree on what to eat or drink but can definitely agree on having a good time together.

2411 Desoto Ave.
912-417-3001, starlandyard.com

RIVER STREET SWEETS®

Celebrating 50 sweet years in business

There's something about walking into a candy store that fills everyone with childlike wonder. River Street Sweets® is a name synonymous with Savannah and gourmet Southern sweets, thanks to 50 years of the Strickland family making their world-famous pralines; saltwater taffy; crunchy, hand-stretched peanut brittle; and homemade pecan pies. It's one of the first stops tourists make when they arrive in the Hostess City of the South, and it's no surprise the holidays are their busiest time of year.

The aroma wafting from the candy store's open doors invites you inside off the cobblestone street, where you're greeted by a symphony of bliss: happy candymakers offering warm samples of melt-in-your-mouth pralines, stirring big batches of glazed pecans in huge copper kettles, a 100-year-old saltwater taffy machine in action, and a nostalgic choo choo train circling inside. Clear cases filled with Chocolate Bear Claws®, fudge, log rolls, caramel candy apples, and rice crispy treats beckon you closer, while many convenient prepackaged treats line the shop's shelves.

The bright red awning with four flagpoles and big white letters along River Street is hard to miss. Fresh greenery flanks each entrance, and tables and chairs welcome guests to rest on the sidewalk and take in the beautiful Savannah River views. The popular candy store is owned and operated by siblings, Tim and Jennifer Strickland, but the business didn't originally begin as a candy store.

Back in 1973, Tim and Jennifer's parents, Stan and Pam, owned the Cotton Bale, a gift shop on historic River Street. A trip to the Atlanta Gift Market trade show would introduce 11-year-old Tim to a fudge pot, piquing his curiosity, and he would beg his parents

Left: The bright red awning of River Street Sweets® has been a beacon for visitors and tourists for more than 50 years. *Center:* Siblings and owners Tim (left) and Jennifer (right) Strickland. *Right:* River Street Sweets® World Famous Pralines® are made with butter, cream, sugar, and lots of Georgia pecans. They are the largest producer of World Famous Pralines® in the country. All photos courtesy of River Street Sweets®.

to put it in their shop. Reluctantly, they agreed, and on St. Patrick's Day a week later, his sister Jennifer would make the first batch of chocolate mint fudge. "The fudge sold like crazy, and it soon became obvious that candy was much more popular than knickknacks and Christmas ornaments," according to an excerpt on the River Street Sweets® website. Soon after, River Street Sweets® was born and today is the oldest candy store in the city, with no sign of slowing down.

In addition to the original River Street location, the candy shop has expanded to multiple other areas of the city and in 2016 began to franchise River Street Sweets®—Savannah's Candy Kitchen throughout the Southeast. Pay them a visit and savor every sweet moment!

13 E River St.
912-234-4608

4515 Habersham St.,
Ste. 201
912-201-3654

32 E Broughton St.
912-349-3884

riverstreetsweets.com

River Street Sweets® is one of United Parcel Service's biggest shippers in Savannah. Their sweets are available for shipping nationwide and all over the world.

SPANKY'S PIZZA GALLEY & SALOON

Home of the original chicken finger

The world's first chicken finger happened right here in the Hostess City.

Many restaurants have that one dish that defines them, the one that visitors return for time and again, like the fried chicken at Mrs. Wilkes' Dining Room, the catfish at Love's Seafood & Steaks, or the pralines at River Street Sweets®. For Spanky's Pizza Galley & Saloon, it's the specially seasoned and battered fried chicken fingers. While chicken fingers may seem all too common these days, Spanky's chicken fingers are something special, not only because they're delicious, but because the owners invented the concept.

Family owned and operated since December of 1976, Spanky's is "where the finger lickin' all began," according to Ansley Williams and brothers Dusty and Alben Yarbrough, originally from Thomaston, Georgia. More than 40 years ago, the three business owners pooled their resources to open the original Spanky's on River Street with the intention of serving the best pizza and half-pound burgers. And that's when the magic happened. A chicken breast they were testing for a sandwich on the menu was too big for the bun. That's when Alben trimmed the edges, fried them up, and made culinary history by giving the world its very

In 2019, on a visit to Savannah, *Southern Living* reported that Spanky's Pizza Galley & Saloon had "the best chicken tenders we've ever tasted." High praise! Spanky's is a part of Live Oak Restaurant Group, which includes Tubby's Tank House, Fiddler's Crab House and Oyster Bar, Molly McGuire's, and Dub's Pub.

Left: Voted "Best bar food in Savannah," Spanky's nachos top the list. *Center:* The original owners (from left) of Spanky's—Dusty Yarbrough, Alben Yarbrough, and Ansley Williams—all grew up as best friends going to school and playing football together in Thomaston, Georgia. *Right:* All pizzas are available in two sizes: personal eight-inch and shareable 14-inch. All photos courtesy of Live Oak Restaurant Group.

first chicken finger. To prove it, they even have an official designation from the United States Congressional Record at the bar.

In addition to Spanky's original chicken fingers, there's one more item on the menu that you can't find anywhere else, and that's Spanky's Spuds. Hand-battered, deep-fried potatoes sliced round, they're extra crispy and perfect for dipping in the restaurant's signature honey horseradish sauce. Local patrons say once you've had them, you'll never go back to eating french fries again.

When it comes to pizza, each one is prepared from scratch and cooked to order with Spanky's freshly made dough and sauce. Try the Spanky's Special, featuring a combination of cheeses, peppers, onions, and four different meats. Fat Cat Platters are for those with extra-large appetites; the surf and turf or fish and chips may suit your fancy. Spanky's is located on the west end of River Street; look for the long yellow-and-white-striped awning and the big black planter boxes filled with friendly flowers to welcome you in.

At Spanky's they believe sharing a good meal with family and friends is one of life's greatest joys. Here, you'll never meet a stranger, and they'll "surely save you a seat where Savannah's greatest characters eat!"

Spanky's Pizza Galley & Saloon
317 E River St.
912-236-3009, spankysriverstreet.com

Spanky's
308 Mall Way
1605 Strand Ave., Tybee Island
1221 E Hwy. 80, Pooler
spankysgang.com

THE GREY

Simultaneously familiar and elevated

You may have seen this restaurant featured in the popular Netflix documentary *Chef's Table*, or perhaps you've heard of its two-time James Beard Award–winning chef. Since its opening in December of 2014, The Grey has received many national accolades, among them Eater's "Restaurant of the Year," *Food & Wine*'s "World's Best Restaurants," and *Esquire*'s "Best Bars in America." With articles featured in the *Wall Street Journal*, the *New York Times*, and *Southern Living*, it's no wonder everyone is talking about the renovated, once-segregated Greyhound-bus-station-turned-hit-restaurant. The Grey is the brainchild of two New Yorkers, John O. Morisano (Johno), managing partner, and Mashama Bailey, executive chef and partner. The two met and immediately bonded over shared views on what makes for delicious food, convinced they could tackle the challenge of opening a restaurant together.

The menus, offered for dinner and brunch, are structured around the seasonality of the region: dynamic and varied. Mashama, who describes her style of cooking as "old English American," enjoys taking traditional, comforting ingredients and updating them for interest and approachability. With an inclination toward regional produce, seafood, and meats, she creates dishes that are deeply flavorful, layered, and soulful. The Chicken Country Captain is a slowly braised whole fryer chicken in a rich broth flavored with curried spices and served with thick sourdough slices for sopping up the sauce. East and West Coast varieties of oysters are available raw, and for brunch, biscuits and gravy are served alongside country ham, poached eggs, and red-eye gravy.

After a two-year, multimillion-dollar renovation with a focus on the preservation of the building, the old Greyhound bus station was

Left: John O. Morisano, managing partner, and Mashama Bailey, executive chef and partner, are the visionaries behind The Grey. *Center:* The Chicken Country Captain garnished with almonds and fresh parsley. Photo courtesy of Cedric Smith. *Right:* Parking for The Grey is on-street or in a nearby parking garage. Arrive early to find a spot.

fully restored to its original luster, and today includes several distinct dining areas: the front diner bar, a large dining room, a private dining room, and a wine cellar. Each area has its own story, sparking thoughtful dinner conversation and an appreciation for progress. The designers describe the 1960s-inspired interior as "Art Deco meets transportational industrial," with custom furniture and decorative lighting. Many of the original bus-station elements are part of the restaurant today, such as the big plate-glass window visible from the sidewalk and the pink terrazzo floors.

As the website so eloquently states, "The Grey continues the building's long tradition of transporting people to a destination, but that destination is now one of elevated hospitality and intrinsic satisfaction."

Reservations are recommended. Dining room dress code is dressy casual, with no gym or beachwear, please.

109 Martin Luther King Jr. Blvd.
912-662-5999, thegreyrestaurant.com

The Grey is expanding internationally, opening its newest restaurant in Paris in 2024, marking a historic moment in American and French culinary exchange.

ELIZABETH ON 37TH

Fine Southern coastal cuisine

Exactly 37 blocks south of the city's riverfront, in an elegant Victorian mansion, is Elizabeth on 37th, aptly named for the late award-winning Chef Elizabeth Terry. A trailblazer for women in culinary arts, Elizabeth paved the way for locally sourced food prepared with intention and presented with gusto. Known for its Southern hospitality, fine coastal cuisine, and well-appointed wines, the restaurant is now owned by Greg and Gary Butch, and the kitchen is expertly run by husband-and-wife Executive Chefs Kelly Yambor and Jeremy Diehl.

After the dilapidated home was renovated in May of 1981, Elizabeth on 37th transformed the city's culinary landscape. Upon arrival, you'll walk the brick pathway and enter the restaurant through fragrant herb gardens planted by Chef Terry—herbs from the garden are used in many of the recipes. Historic original paintings, fresh flowers, and ceramics decorate the interior. White tablecloths and antique rugs fill the colorful 6,000-square-foot space, complete with hardwood floors, fireplaces, and grand architectural details.

An article written by food writer Martha Nesbit published in the *Savannah Morning News* shortly after Chef Terry's passing expounds on her legacy:

> *Elizabeth's story was unique. She was a female in a profession where there were few females. She was a self-taught chef in a field where credentials are important. And she insisted on putting family first in a profession that demands long hours. She exhibited a confidence in her abilities in the kitchen that she attributes to her mother, Nanee Bennett, who told her she could do anything.*

Left: Spicy Savannah red rice with Georgia shrimp and Half Moon River clams, sausage, grouper, and okra. *Right:* Elizabeth on 37th has been a favorite fine-dining destination in Savannah since 1981.

That confidence would translate well for Elizabeth on 37th. Soon after the restaurant opened, it gained national attention from acclaimed sources such as *Gourmet* magazine, *Food & Wine*, and *Bon Appétit*. The James Beard Foundation recognized Chef Terry on more than one occasion: in 1987, she was the first woman chef to cook for the foundation as a Rising Star, and in 1995, she earned the prestigious James Beard Award for Best Chef Southeast. As the restaurant grew in popularity, her career would include numerous accolades, which still inspire the team's traditional and innovative dishes today.

The Chef's Tasting Menu changes seasonally and features seven courses, including optional wine pairings. Ingredients are sourced locally, including sweet Georgia shrimp, fresh flounder, and black sea bass. In the summertime, for example, Georgia peach and blueberry cobbler may be featured for dessert, as might a triple chocolate brownie.

105 E 37th St.
912-236-5547, elizabethon37th.net

Parking is available on 37th Street in front of the restaurant, across the street.

GREEN TRUCK NEIGHBORHOOD PUB

Savannah's grass-fed burger joint

Josh Yates didn't set out to own a hamburger joint. About five years after graduating from the Georgia Institute of Technology, he worked as an engineer in an auto parts factory making brake pads. One day, the plant closed, and he found himself without a job.

"The opportunity was, do I continue to look for another job? My specialty was in manufacturing, which was a poor pick, because it was a shrinking field, unless I wanted to move to China or pursue something else," he says. And luckily for Savannahians, he chose the latter. He decided to attend graduate school to earn a business degree. During the day, he worked in cafés and bakeries. He had worked in restaurants before and enjoyed the energy and pace. "My father had a BBQ stand," he says. "He was always an entrepreneur; I always liked that, and I liked the restaurant business."

Originally from DeLand, Florida, Josh and his wife, Whitney, also a Georgia Tech graduate, moved to Savannah when Whitney was offered a job. "It kind of reminded us of home a little bit," he says. "A lot of the flora and fauna are more similar to Florida here than in Atlanta—big Spanish moss and live oaks," he says. In an up-and-coming neighborhood in Midtown Savannah, they found a former Crispy Chick for rent, which had been sitting empty for a year. Josh and Whitney leased the space, and Green Truck Neighborhood Pub was born in 2010.

The restaurant has earned high praise for its grass-fed, all-natural, hormone-free beef sourced from Hunter Cattle Company. Voted "Best Burger" and "Best Fries" in Savannah by locals consecutively for more than a decade, the menu also features sandwiches, salads, and desserts.

Top left: Owners Josh and Whitney Yates. Photo courtesy of Siobhan Egan for Paprika Southern. *Above left:* The Rustico, one of the most popular burgers on the menu, is made with goat cheese, balsamic caramelized onions, roasted red peppers, and fresh basil. Photo courtesy of Siobhan Egan for Paprika Southern. *Above center:* Take your burger to the next level with Green Truck's made-from-scratch tomato ketchup. Photo courtesy of Siobhan Egan for Paprika Southern. *Top right:* Got an appetite? The Whole Farm comes with bacon, cheddar, and a fried egg! Photo courtesy of Siobhan Egan for Paprika Southern. *Above right:* Josh Yates stands outside next to the restaurant's namesake, a 1965 Chevy stepside.

Everything is handmade, from the crispy hand cut-fries to the ketchup, pimento cheese, salad dressings, and veggie patties. They serve beers from small American craft brewers owned and operated in the US.

As for the namesake, there is an actual green truck—a 1965 Chevy stepside Josh rebuilt by hand. "I take it every Saturday to the Forsyth Farmers Market, where we pick up a lot of vegetables, and pecans too for our homemade pies," he says. "When it came time to name the restaurant, we decided to use my truck as a mascot—a back-to-basics emblem of what we're doing here."

2430 Habersham St.
912-234-5885, greentruckpub.com

Green Truck Neighborhood Pub does not take reservations or call-ahead seating. There may be a short wait during peak hours, but it's well worth it.

FINCHES SANDWICHES & SUNDRIES

Good food on the fly

In a 1950s gas station in the small town of Thunderbolt, you'll find Finches Sandwiches & Sundries, an eclectic and retro "happy little sandwich shop" owned by Jamie Pleta and Rebecca Gawley. The shop is known for serving good food on the fly in the form of gourmet breakfast and lunch sandwiches, soups, salads, and desserts.

Jamie and Rebecca met while working as team members at a luxury hotel in downtown Savannah. They played complementing roles in the food and beverage side of the same hospitality group, Rebecca dabbling in the wine program and Jamie working as a restaurant manager. During the pandemic, those roles came to an end, leading them to eventually dream up a concept of their own.

Finches Sandwiches & Sundries opened in December of 2020, first in a 700-square-foot former mechanics shop, a blue cement building with a 300-square-foot kitchen. They only offered counter service at the time, but as business grew, so did their space. They acquired the gas station next door, and today the entire mechanics shop has become the kitchen, while the gas station serves as front-of-house.

"As a small business, we budgeted our growth in phases, first outfitting the exterior with picnic tables and Astroturf and still running service through the mechanics shop," says Rebecca. "Once we occupied both properties, we set up mess-hall-style dining tables

Finches Sandwiches & Sundries is open for weekday lunch and weekend brunch.

Left: The Nookie, with deli-sliced turkey, house-made tomato relish, melted cheddar, sriracha mayo, and shredded lettuce on a Hawaiian roll. *Center:* Owners Jamie Pleta (left) and Rebecca Gawley (right). *Right:* The inside of the gas station was formerly an Airbnb and has been converted to a retail space. All photos courtesy of Finches Sandwiches & Sundries.

and added a fantastical outdoor mural of finches, our namesake bird." The mural was created by Kipper Millsap, whose iconic work is scattered on many downtown Savannah landmarks.

Among their most popular menu items is the Millennials Toast, made with toasted Auspicious Bakery Co. ciabatta, smashed avocado, cream cheese, and allspiced almonds. Try it with a side of Old Bay–dusted tots and cool off with Leopold's Ice Cream or a root beer float for dessert.

In addition to their daily-changing menu, Finches has shelves stocked with a thoughtfully curated selection of vintage candies, local merchandise, and nostalgic products that give a nod to yesteryear. "We believe Finches is a community space that stretches way beyond gourmet sandwiches," says Rebecca. "While we set out to be an eatery, what we became was a hub for creators, entrepreneurs, fundraisers, and activism. There are many things you learn as a business owner, but our greatest lesson in owning a lunch joint is that most differences can be set aside over a good sandwich."

2600 Mechanics Ave., Thunderbolt
912-509-8053, @finches.sandwiches

SWEET SPICE RESTAURANT

Jamaican us hungry

Situated on the corner of 70th Street and Waters Avenue on the end of a small strip mall you'll find Sweet Spice Restaurant, a no-frills Jamaican eatery serving hearty portions. Given a window of opportunity, Chef Donavon Smith, a native of Westmoreland, Jamaica, seized the moment. Much to his surprise, he realized that no one was serving the flavors of his hometown in the Hostess City of the South. In 2011, Sweet Spice Restaurant opened its doors.

Born into a family of five, Donavon grew up cooking by his mother's side and had mastered the traditional dishes of her kitchen by the time he was 12. Known for serving authentic "Caribbean and American delights," Sweet Spice Restaurant features a variety of island flavors, such as oxtails, tender curry goat, and plantains. Peas and rice are a common side dish, a nod to one of Donavon's favorite childhood food memories. As a boy, he would often eat a combination of the two with coconut milk and brown stew chicken. Yelp reviewers have a favorite go-to dish: jerk chicken seasoned with thyme, allspice, and bonnet peppers, a favorite of Donavon's today. As for the "American delights," Donavon has included a few classic, familiar dishes on the menu, such as macaroni and cheese and red velvet cake. If you've never been, a great way to enjoy a variety of Jamaican staples is by ordering the Sweet Spice Sampler, a play on the meat and three, which comes with three meats, a starch, and a vegetable. Everyone will recognize the Bob Marley burrito, served open-faced and piled high with grilled chicken and your choice of vegetables.

Though quaint, the mom-and-pop shop offers indoor and outdoor seating in a friendly, colorful, and lively atmosphere. Reggae music sets the mood, and each time the door swings open, "Welcome to Sweet Spice, where everything is nice!" is the standard, happy greeting.

Left: Chef Donavon Smith. Photo courtesy of Jessica Leigh Lebos for Connect Savannah. *Top center:* Escovitch fish is a Caribbean dish of fried fish marinated in a tangy vinegar sauce with vegetables and spices. Photo courtesy of Sweet Spice Restaurant. *Above center:* Sweet Spice curried shrimp with white rice and corn. Photo courtesy of Sweet Spice Restaurant. *Right:* Sweet Spice food trucks are available to cater weddings, birthdays, and anniversaries. Photo courtesy of Sweet Spice Restaurant.

With high rankings on Yelp and Tripadvisor, the family-owned-and-operated restaurant has grown from one location to two since its opening, with the addition of food trucks. Painted in the unmistakable bright gold and green colors of the Jamaican flag, the food trucks serve Savannah and the surrounding area, and they can be easily spotted at community events.

Bailee A. said it best in a five-star online Yelp review: "This place is flavorful. Everything is fresh and made with love. If you're looking for good authentic island cuisine, this is your place. Worth every penny!"

5515 Waters Ave.
1024 W US Hwy. 80, Pooler
912-335-8146, sweetspicesavannah.net

Sweet Spice Restaurant has a dedicated parking area directly in front of the business.

VINNIE VAN GOGO'S

Slinging Neapolitan pies since 1991

In a white brick building at the corner of Montgomery and West Bryan Streets in City Market, there's a well-known pizza joint that's been slinging New York–style pies since 1991. Vinnie Van GoGo's opened in February that year, during a time when there weren't many affordable places to dine downtown. Tourism was picking up, and the Savannah College of Art and Design was growing, purchasing many of the city's abandoned buildings and bringing with it lots of hungry art students. Vinnie Van GoGo's was ready to feed them. The restaurant's namesake and logo, which depicts Van Gogh in a white chef's hat with a notoriously large slice of pizza, are cleverly inspired by famous Dutch painter Vincent van Gogh.

Vinnie's serves up Neapolitan-style pizzas, made with a thin, hearty crust, rich marinara sauce, and grated parmesan and mozzarella cheeses. You can order a whole pie—a 14-inch medium or an 18-inch large—or pizza by the slice. Make no mistake, these are not your average slices. One slice at Vinnie's is more like two anywhere else. An array of vegetable and meat toppings are available, from artichokes and broccoli to hamburger and anchovies. The menu also features calzones made with ricotta and mozzarella cheeses, garlic, and herbs wrapped in dough and baked golden brown. For those craving something green with your pie, a simple spinach salad is offered with Italian vinaigrette dressing on the side. There are plenty of local beers on draft, such as Moon River and Southbound Brewing's Hop'lin IPA.

The vibe inside Vinnie's is super eclectic. Low-slung white clapboard ceilings, a long wooden bar, and exposed brick walls strung with white lights are decorated with bygone concert posters and

Left: On any given day, Vinnie Van GoGo's outdoor patio is full of hungry patrons. *Right:* A medium 14-inch pie with mushrooms, olives, and pepperoni on one half, and on the other half pepperoni and sun-dried tomatoes.

framed photographs of past celebrity visitors. A few highboy tables are available near the bar, where pizza makers toss dough into the air and kitschy bumper stickers cover the beverage cooler. The majority of seating is outdoors, along the covered and pet-friendly patio.

For many years, Vinnie Van GoGo's only accepted cash as payment, but they recently began accepting cards as well. During peak tourist season, if the restaurant is unable to seat your party, consider ordering a pizza to go and finding a shady spot to eat it under the Spanish moss–covered oak trees on a bench in City Market or nearby Franklin Square.

317 W Bryan St.
912-233-6394, vinnievangogo.com

If you're visiting Savannah, here's a fun fact: Vinnie's delivers its pizzas to the downtown area on bicycles.

GLO'S COFFEE CORNER

Coffee and community

Just across the Little Ogeechee River, only 14 miles southwest of downtown Savannah, there's a quiet, coastal suburban community known as Georgetown with sweeping Spanish moss–covered oak trees and a small-town neighborhood vibe all its own. Every small town needs a quaint coffee shop, and since 2018, Glo's Coffee Corner has been the quintessential community-centric spot.

It's conveniently located a short drive from I-95, but if you didn't know it was there, you might miss it. Positioned on the end of a strip mall with a few other restaurants and a grocery store, Glo's Coffee Corner serves breakfast and lunch daily, along with local Cup to Cup Coffee Roasters small-batch coffee, teas, and classic milkshakes. All the coffee drinks you might expect are on the menu—lattes, caramel macchiatos, and mochas—but the Barista Specials change with the season. In the summertime, selections such as the Beach Party Latte feature flavors of peach and white chocolate, and the Coconut Island is made with strawberry, coconut, and dark chocolate.

A small pastry case is filled with a charming selection of enticing baked goods, including cinnamon rolls and donuts. For lunch, salads and panini melts are made fresh to order and sandwiches are served with a small side, such as the mac and cheese made with an in-house cheese sauce and bacon.

"I love everything about Glo's," says Caroline Farrar, a regular customer. "I really appreciate that they take many different dietary needs into consideration with their menu. They have vegan and gluten-free food options, as well as different types of milk for people who need dairy-free drinks. Their coffee is great (especially the Almond Joy Latte), but the food is amazing. I haven't tried anything from Glo's that I didn't like. Their soups are also fabulous."

Left: Glo's Coffee Corner offers indoor and outdoor patio seating. *Center left:* The Caprese Panini Melt with fresh tomatoes, mozzarella, spinach and basil pesto, and a side of mac and cheese with bacon. *Center right:* A blueberry muffin and lavender latte inside the bright and happy dining area. *Right:* A breakfast croissant sandwich with a side of fresh fruit in the morning light. Photo courtesy of Glo's Coffee Corner.

In addition to a delicious menu, Glo's Coffee Corner prides itself on being a special place to gather with friends and family. Toward the back of the eatery, there's a dedicated Kid's Corner with books and toys for babies and toddlers. Board games and a shared library of books offer customers fun activities. The coffee shop doubles as a mini marketplace for local makers, with earrings, illustrated greeting cards, and French soap for sale. Local artists can feature their work on the walls, and a market shelf showcases small businesses. If you're short on time, Glo's Coffee Corner offers a drive-through window. Get a jump start on your order by calling ahead before pickup.

1040 King George Blvd., #60
912-777-5618, facebook.com/gloscoffee

Glo's Coffee Corner offers a hero's discount for members of the military, after-school free snacks for kids, art classes, and a book club. They are a cashless business, accepting card payment and Venmo only.

SAVANNAH COFFEE ROASTERS

Café and bistro since 1909

Savannah Coffee Roasters is not your average coffee shop. Located in the Historic District on bustling West Liberty Street, this modern café and bistro with Australian influences has been crafting perfect cups of coffee for more than 100 years, and their breakfast and lunch menus are just as delicious as the coffee. Savannah Coffee Roasters was established in 1909 by Edgar R. Morrison, a 21-year-old under the tutelage of his entrepreneurial father. The first location was on Bay Street. In the mid-1800s, Edgar's father, David Morrison, owned DJ Morrison and Sons Dry Grocers on West Broughton Street in Savannah.

Today the popular coffee shop is owned and operated by the Collins family—Lori Collins is president and CEO, and her son, Jason Collins, serves as chief operating officer. Carrying on Edgar's love for coffee, the family believes in hand-roasting small batches of coffee fresh, using only the best Arabica beans. Prior to opening their current location, the family business operated for 20 years at Savannah's Oglethorpe Mall roasting coffee and baking cookies. "Our famous Savannah Blend is 30 years old," says Lori. "Savannah Pecan is one of our most popular coffees, and Savannah Seduction is enjoyed in Milan, Italy."

Savannah Coffee Roasters' Captain's Choice, a medium-roasted, smooth, and well-balanced blend made with a mixture of dark and medium roast Arabica beans, was named a Top 10 Coffee in the US by *Consumer Reports,* a huge recognition for this small, artisanal manufacturer!

Top left: The Ultimate Grilled Cheese sandwich is made with ciabatta bread, cheddar, swiss, and a parmesan dijon sauce, served with chips. *Above left:* The menu features a wide variety of seasonal soups and salads, such as the sweet potato salad, with baby greens, roasted sweet potatoes, candied walnuts, and feta cheese. *Right:* Lori Collins, president and CEO of Savannah Coffee Roasters. Photo courtesy of Savannah Coffee Roasters.

On staff is roastmaster Nigel Gardner, head roaster, who has been with the team since 2012. He began roasting coffee as a hobby, learning the intricacies of each style: drip coffee, French press, then espresso, and today relies on that knowledge to draw out the subtle nuances of flavor hidden in every bean. Also on the team is Executive Chef Timothy Michael from Baltimore, Maryland. Chef Timothy arrives daily at 4 a.m. to begin baking fresh pastries, sweets, cakes, and pies to fill the delightful and ever-evolving pastry case.

When you step inside Savannah Coffee Roasters, the concrete floors signal its unique 5,000-square-foot working factory setting, and the exposed brick walls and burlap table coverings create a warm and welcoming atmosphere. Just above the coffee shop is the Morrison Room, a sizable, furnished space available to the community for corporate meetings.

"Take the drive, come and say hello, and watch the coffee roast," says Lori. "Enjoy a cuppa and experience Southern hospitality, and the heady scents of freshly roasted coffee."

215 W Liberty St.
912-352-2994, savannahcoffee.com

YIA YIA'S KITCHEN & MARKETPLACE

Authentic Greek food

The Stathopoulos family is bringing a taste of Kalamata—the second most popular seaside city in Southern Greece, renowned for Kalamata olive oil and olives—to Savannah. For more than nine years, Yia Yia's Kitchen & Marketplace at the corner of 48th and Habersham Streets in the popular Ardsley Park neighborhood has served as the city's authentic Greek ethnic-style bakery and deli, offering imported foods, cheeses, beer, and wine. They are also known for their ice cream, Greek coffee, and pastries, such as baklava.

"Yia Yia is actually Greek for grandmother," says Atha Stathopoulos, manager, and son of owners Stathy and Penny Stathopoulos. "When you think of Grandma's kitchen, you think of good food." A native Savannahian and retired safety manager with the Georgia Ports Authority, Stathy opened the business with his wife, Penny, in June of 2014. "I was born and raised here; my dad was born and raised here," says Atha. "Both of my grandparents on my dad's side actually came over on the boat from Greece."

As a volunteer for Savannah's Greek Festival hosted by St. Paul's Greek Orthodox Church for many years, Stathy listened to the feedback and realized people wanted their Greek food fix more often than once a year. Other ethnic markets in Savannah existed, such as Asian places, but there was not a Greek or Mediterranean market. As a first-generation Greek, Stathy decided to bring a taste of his heritage to his hometown.

All of the authentic baked goods are imported from Hellas Bakery in Tarpon Springs, Florida, boasting the highest percentage of Greek Americans of any city in the US. Known for their rich and

Left: Yia Yia's chicken souvlaki gyro, a bestseller and Atha's favorite menu item. Photo courtesy of Yia Yia's. *Center:* Atha Stathopoulos and Samantha Williams, managers of Yia Yia's. *Right:* A holiday baklava sampler platter. Photo courtesy of Yia Yia's.

buttery pastries and specialty desserts, such as baklava cheesecake and baklava Napoleon (cream-filled baklava), Hellas's products are baked fresh daily with only the finest ingredients. The menu also features specialty Greek entrées, such as moussaka (a casserole) and pastitsio (lasagna), salads, sandwiches, hot dogs, and Kronos gyros.

Atha says what makes Yia Yia's unique is its authenticity, especially when it comes to the ingredients in common sauces, such as tzatziki. "A lot of places, whenever they make tzatziki, they use sour cream, where tzatziki is traditionally made with yogurt," he says. "We use a yogurt Skotidakis brand where the family is based up in Canada. They have their own goats and a goat dairy farm. They're making it themselves."

3113 Habersham St.
912-200-3796, yiayiasav.com

With indoor and outdoor seating, Yia Yia's Kitchen & Marketplace offers dine-in, delivery, take-out, and catering.

BELLA'S ITALIAN CAFE

Where Savannah eats Italian

For Jim and Joyce Shanks, the restaurant business is a calling. The husband-and-wife team opened Bella's Italian Cafe in the trendy Habersham Village of midtown Savannah in August of 1993. For more than 30 years, their little Italian café has been "where Savannah eats Italian." Ask anyone local what they're known for, and the answer will be the breadsticks.

Served in charming terra-cotta pots, the breadsticks are soft and warm, brought to the table first along with a rich marinara sauce and a softened herb butter. One bite grabs your attention for what's to come. "Those were my dad's invention, and he hit the nail on the head," says Reina Shanks, daughter of the owners and general manager of Bella's. The chicken parmesan baked with marinara and melted cheeses is by far the most popular dish, and two others, baked ziti with sausage and lasagna, are close behind. The restaurant is named after Joyce's grandmother Bella, which means "beautiful" in Italian, and many of the recipes served in the restaurant today—such as the manicotti and pasta e fagioli (pasta and bean soup)—were inspired by Bella and her husband, William.

Jim and Joyce, originally from New York, grew up down the street from each other and attended grade school together. After college, Jim was living in Virginia and Joyce had opened her first restaurant in Philadelphia. "A few life events later, we were married and traveling Europe together for the next two years, learning about cuisine and cooking," says Joyce. This experience only enhanced Joyce's upbringing next to her Italian mother and grandmother in the kitchen. When they returned to the States, they moved to Atlanta, where they both worked for a large restaurant group, which eventually landed them in Savannah.

"We used to come to Savannah for a quick getaway, and quickly fell in love," she says. At the time, the couple realized the city only

Top left: Spaghetti and meatballs. *Above left:* Limoncello cake is a lemon-infused sponge cake with Italian mascarpone, topped with blueberry compote. *Top center:* Jim (right) and Joyce (left) Shanks, owners. Photo courtesy of Bella's Italian Cafe. *Above center:* Angel hair garlic and oil with shrimp, scallops, and sun-dried tomatoes. *Right:* The famous breadsticks at Bella's, served with marinara and herb butter.

had one Italian restaurant. "We thought we could offer a menu and concept Savannah would embrace," said Joyce. "It did just that."

For their daughter Reina, the couple's success has been inspiring. "I have watched my parents build this restaurant from the ground up since I was three," she says. "The recipes haven't changed, and today the dining room is full of community, family, and history. To see my parents turn this little Italian joint into an iconic part of local Savannah living makes me so proud of them and everything they did to get here."

4420 Habersham St.
912-354-4005, bellascafe.com

Bella's accepts reservations for parties of six or more. Parking is available in front of the restaurant and in the designated parking area just south of the restaurant.

DRIFTAWAY CAFÉ

Casual coastal cuisine

On September 10, 2001, Robyn Quattlebaum invited friends and family to dine in his brand-new restaurant, set to open the very next day, for a dry run to make sure the team had all of their systems and procedures in place. With nervous energy before the opening, he stayed up all night polishing and prepping, getting ready to open the doors to the public after an entire summer of remodeling the Driftaway Café.

"I turned on the televisions in the bar area the morning of September 11, 2001, and much to my shock, all stations were broadcasting the footage of that first plane crashing into the World Trade Center," he says. "My staff had begun arriving for our grand opening, as that second plane came sailing in." Robyn decided then and there that September 11, this terrible day for all Americans, would not be their anniversary. They waited a few days and opened on September 14. "I never thought I'd see a more difficult year than our first year in business," he says. "Then 2020 comes along and says, 'Hold my beer, watch this.'" Sales were down 73 percent in 2020 from the year before.

Despite the pandemic and other challenges, the Driftaway Café, which he owns with his wife, Michele, is now celebrating more than 22 years in business. Located in the coastal community of Sandfly, near Isle of Hope, just a bike ride away from where Robyn grew up on picturesque Bluff Drive, the Driftaway is known for its gourmet seafood dishes sourced fresh from the Atlantic. Zesty calamari, tender tuna bites, and the popular firecracker shrimp tacos fill the menu featuring brunch, lunch, and dinner selections.

Enjoy live music often on the porch, indoor and outdoor seating, and a large gravel parking area.

Top left: The corned beef hash is a brunch dish featuring sliced corned beef (not out of the can) on top of homestyle potatoes, with poached eggs and hollandaise. *Above left:* A hand-painted mural surrounds the restaurant, featuring local shrimp boats, seagulls, wild herons and Spanish moss–covered oak trees. *Top right:* Lavern Baker, a cook at Driftaway Café for nearly five years, and owner Robyn Quattlebaum. *Above right:* Jamaican French toast with thick-sliced Texas toast dredged in dark rum and cinnamon batter, served with crispy bacon and syrup.

A breathtaking hand-painted mural depicting scenes of the Georgia coast and local shrimp boats surrounds the dining room. Comfortable booths line a large window overlooking a babbling brook with turtles and other wildlife.

The pulse of hospitality has flowed through Robyn's veins since 1979, when he took his first restaurant job making salads and washing dishes. Throughout his career, he climbed the ranks, holding nearly every back-of-house and front-of-house position in various restaurants. "To this day, nothing can make me happier than a dining room full of people enjoying a good meal," he says.

When it comes to dining out, Savannah offers many choices, but there's one thing that Robyn says sets Driftaway Café apart. "We understand the definition of hospitality, which is the sincere and genuine welcome, reception, and entertainment of friends, family, and strangers alike."

7400 Skidaway Rd.
912-303-0999, driftawaycafe.com

ARDSLEY STATION

Food. Drink. Community.

In Ardsley Station's first two years of business in the Starland district, locals consistently voted the neighborhood eatery "Best Overall Restaurant" and "Best Wait Staff," two accolades that directly reflect their community-centric and service-minded culture. Featuring approachable American cuisine, their menu is part coastal Northeast and part Pacific Northwest, a blend of backgrounds and influences the owners and executive chef together bring to the table.

Tyler and Kara Kopkas, originally from Seattle, own the restaurant with Kara's aunt and uncle Steve and Mary Paschall, retired Upstate New Yorkers who permanently moved to Savannah during the pandemic. Executive Chef Dustin Rickers is from Bath, Maine, and has a background in coastal fine dining. "There's a lot of coastal influence—North, South, and West—that make up our menu," says Tyler. "It is very Southern, but in our own unique way."

The unpretentious philosophy behind Ardsley Station centers on three ideas that have a symbiotic relationship: food, drink, and community. "That was always the vision for this place," Tyler says. "We want people to get that feeling that they're comfortable, and that this is an extension of their dining room."

Ardsley Station offers weekend brunch along with lunch and dinner seven days a week. One crowd-pleasing dish, which Tyler refers to as the "caviar of the South," is pimento cheese bruschetta made with white cheddar and served with local peaches in the summertime and red pepper jelly. The menu also showcases a nightly fin fish and day-boat catch highlighting the native fish in coastal Georgia such as red snapper, grouper, sheepshead, mahi, and swordfish. "Trying to think holistically, everything we bring in the door here is within 250 to 300 miles," says Tyler. As part of its ethos

Left: Deviled eggs with house-made, stone-ground mustard and paprika. *Top center:* Get Smashed Station Libation features vodka, limoncello, and seasonal fruit, and pairs well with the Buffalo chicken sandwich and crispy fries. *Above center:* In addition to a variety of good food, enjoy indoor and outdoor seating, covered patio with a retractable roof, firepit, and TVs. *Right:* Co-owner Tyler Kopkas with Executive Chef Dustin Rickers. All photos courtesy of A Different Light Photography.

of giving back to the community, the restaurant sources high-quality ingredients from many specially selected farms and vendors. The menu changes seasonally.

For Ardsley Station, supporting local doesn't just mean by way of ingredients. On the third Tuesday of every month, in partnership with a Savannah marketing company, the restaurant hosts "Sips at the Station," a networking event series that spotlights a different nonprofit each month. In just two years they have donated nearly $50,000 to organizations such as the Forsyth Farmers Market, Safe Shelter, Girl Scouts of America, and Habitat for Humanity.

"We have a great team, and I value the culture here more than anything," says Tyler. "It's above everything else."

102 E Victory Dr.
912-777-5888, ardsleystation.com

The team behind Ardsley Station will open a second concept in the spring of 2024. Hog Stompin' BBQ, at 3811 Montgomery St., will offer a modern take on a Southern staple.

EASTERN WHARF

A dining port of call

Anchoring the east end of the Savannah riverfront is Eastern Wharf, a 54-acre residential, retail, and dining destination. With curated shops and an ever-growing portfolio of restaurants, an artisan bakery, and an exquisite rooftop bar, the Park at Eastern Wharf is host to year-round festivals, local food trucks, a cornhole league, and a riverfront concert series.

At Thompson Savannah, a luxury riverfront hotel, is Bar Julian, Savannah's tallest rooftop bar. It's an upscale space to sip craft and spirit-free cocktails where you can take in sweeping views of the Savannah River and enjoy live music. Bar Julian offers a Mediterranean bar menu complete with salads, pizza, and flatbread sandwiches; the arugula salad features lemon, parmesan, and citrus breadcrumbs. Named after the patron saint of hospitality, St. Julian the Hospitaller, Bar Julian embodies the warm hospitality of the Hostess City.

At the helm of Thompson Savannah's baking and pastry program, with a special focus on Stevedore Bakery, is Executive Pastry Chef Noah Whritenour, a New York native and graduate of Johnson & Wales University in Providence, Rhode Island. Offering locally roasted PERC coffee, buttery croissants, artisan breads, and sweet and savory pastries, the menu showcases Southern farmers, such as Columbia, South Carolina–based Anson Mills. Many of the baguettes and loaves are made with Abruzzi rye and buckwheat flour, resulting in a richer,

Other dining options at Eastern Wharf include Latin Chicks; Mint to Be Mojito Bar & Bites; and Honeysuckle Gelato, a North Carolina-based gelato maker. Visit by car or boat! Public dock space and ample parking are available on-site.

Top left: Fleeting specializes in meals inspired by local farmers' markets, seasonal produce, and the Savannah River. *Above left:* Stevedore Bakery offers a variety of hearth breads and handcrafted pastries. *Top center:* Bar Julian's arugula salad with citrus breadcrumbs and the San Marzano pizza. *Top right:* The $600 million mixed-use project broke ground in October of 2018 and has since opened in phases. *Above right:* Squirrel's Pizza sits on the riverfront in The Park at Eastern Wharf.

deeper color and complex flavor from the caramelization of the crust and longer baking times. The sourdough country loaf, perfect for sandwiches and toast, is naturally leavened with a sourdough starter and takes over 48 hours to produce. The menu also features freshly prepared ready-to-go items such as mixed green salads, yogurt parfaits, and whipped feta.

Inside Thompson Savannah is their signature restaurant, Fleeting, which celebrates the bountiful Georgia coast and the rich history of Southern cuisine. The seasonal menu, inspired by the farmers market and its proximity to the Savannah River, features wood-fired meats and seafood such as roasted East Coast oysters and local vegetables. Hyper-seasonal craft cocktails and a curated wine selection complement the menu.

In the heart of Eastern Wharf is Squirrel's Pizza, a stand-alone open-air concept built from shipping containers, with a lively bar serving tavern-style pizza and wings. An outdoor seating area features round picnic tables with umbrellas and Adirondack chairs facing the river. Patio lights strung between palm trees and small gravel crunching underfoot create a beach vibe.

1 Altamaha St.
912-658-4076, easternwharfsavannah.com

CIRCA 1875

A Parisian bistro and pub

Restaurateurs Donald Lubowicki and Jeffrey Downey moved to Savannah from Detroit, working as waiters in some of Savannah's finest restaurants before opening a place of their own. By 2007 they had saved enough to make their dreams come true, opening Circa 1875 as a gastropub. Located in the heart of downtown Savannah on Whitaker Street, just around the corner from the Paris Market and Brocante, the gastropub has expanded to include a Parisian bistro serving classic French cuisine in an authentic old-world setting.

Having worked their entire lives in the restaurant industry, Donald and Jeffrey had each held every position in front-of-house and back-of-house, gaining the experience necessary to own and operate a restaurant. Partners in business since 1991, they bring a flavor all their own to Circa 1875, as reflected in the traditional 19th-century decor and period architectural details lovingly restored to their original beauty. The gastropub features a mahogany bar, intricate tile floors and moldings, and tin-pressed ceiling tiles original to 1875. Reservations are not accepted on the gastropub side of the restaurant; however, the full menu is available.

With "unpretentious French" as their motto, the menu features an extensive wine selection and hors d'oeuvres such as frites (french fries); escargots; and coquilles St. Jacques, a classic dish made with sea scallops, mushrooms, and scallions topped with St. Andre mornay sauce. After

Donald and Jeffrey also own La Scala Ristorante, 119 E 37th St., an authentic fine-dining Italian restaurant set in a restored turn-of-the-century mansion.

Top left: Pull a chair up to the mahogany bar for a beer on tap, or domestic or old-world wine. *Above left:* Ten-ounce New York strip steak and french fried potatoes finished with a red wine demi-glace. *Top right:* Classic crème brûlée garnished with fresh blackberries and mint. *Above right:* An extensive red and white wine list hangs on the wall in the primary dining room, alongside French paintings. All photos courtesy of Circa 1875.

enjoying dinner at Circa 1875, Zack B. from Washington, DC, said in a Yelp review, "We started with their delicious pâté and cheese board, which was expanded to include smoked meats at the suggestion of our waitress . . . It took me right back to vacationing in France and picnicking on the grounds of Versailles!" A popular main course is the truite de ruisseau poêlé, a pan-dressed Carolina brook trout served with glazed carrots and finished with lemon caper brown butter sauce.

Circa 1875 features a private dining space known as the "wine cellar" with exposed brick walls and stained glass windows located on the lower level. Candlelight, white tablecloths, and a single rose vase create a one-of-a-kind ambiance with the space seating up to 27 guests. Designated a Diner's Choice winner on Open Table, which recognizes outstanding restaurants based on feedback from thousands of local diners, Circa 1875 also earned a certificate of excellence from Tripadvisor honoring hospitality businesses that deliver consistently great service across the world.

48 Whitaker St.
912-443-1875, circa1875.com

THE GASLIGHT GROUP

B. Matthew's Eatery, the 5 Spot, Abe's on Lincoln

In 2006, Brian and Jennifer Huskey relocated to Savannah from Knoxville, Tennessee, to establish the Gaslight Group, a collective of hospitality-based businesses that have quickly earned them a reputation for delicious, approachable, family-friendly food in uniquely beautiful settings. Brian comes by his love for the food industry honestly; his mother managed his school cafeteria, and he would go into work with her early in the mornings to help set up for breakfast. Years later, she also managed the concession stand at the University of Tennessee, where Brian worked while earning his college degree. He continued working in the restaurant industry, gaining experience at major chain restaurants, until the opportunity presented itself to purchase his own place.

"We took a leap of faith and uprooted," says Brian. "I quit my job, Jennifer quit her job, and we took our son out of school. I was 39 at the time and felt it was either now or never." Brian's best friend had moved to Savannah first, and once he and Jennifer visited, they too chose to make the Hostess City home. "We decided that Savannah was the kind of community that we would like to support, and we believed they would support the kind of businesses that we wanted to create," he says. As it turns out, they were exactly right.

B. Matthew's Eatery, their flagship restaurant and a popular brunch locale at the corner of Bay and Habersham Streets, offers breakfast, lunch, and dinner menus that feature a variety of traditional and New

The Gaslight Group believes in giving back and reinvesting in the community. In 2022, they donated over $16,000 to more than 50 local nonprofits and organizations.

Left: Abe's on Lincoln at Christmastime. Photo courtesy of David Baez. *Top right:* B. Matthew's Eatery's bourbon bacon burger served with homemade bourbon bacon jam, pepper jack cheese, and fried onions. Photo courtesy of Blake Studwell. *Bottom right:* The 5 Spot is a popular stop for weekend brunch. Photo courtesy of the Gaslight Group.

American–style dishes. Originally constructed in 1854 as a private residence for Hugh Cullen, an Irish immigrant and grocer by trade, the property has performed many functions over the years, including a sailor's boardinghouse, fruit store, and pub. In 2012, with a complete restoration, the Huskeys created the warm and inviting atmosphere it has today with exposed brick and charming architectural details.

Added to the Gaslight Group in 2010 is Abe's on Lincoln, the quintessential local dive bar. Plastered on every wall and the low-slung ceiling are guest drawings on napkins of Abraham Lincoln. Play darts, enjoy local beer on tap, and meet the friendly bartenders who will always keep your glass full.

The 5 Spot Midtown is a casual neighborhood kitchen and bar, serving breakfast, lunch, dinner, and a sought-after happy hour with multiple locations and a food truck. The burgers and salads are the most popular menu items, complete with plenty of vegetarian and vegan options.

B. Matthew's Eatery
325 E Bay St.
912-233-1319

Abe's on Lincoln
17 Lincoln St.
912-349-0525

The 5 Spot

4430 Habersham St.
912-777-3021

7360 Skidaway Rd.
Unit E-1
912-963-1914

3742 Hwy. 17
Richmond Hill
912-200-4480

gaslight-group.com

THE DRAFT ROOM AT BERWICK

Quality. Community. Sports.

The Draft Room at Berwick is not your average sports bar. The casual and inviting family-friendly American restaurant, where employees know your name and order, is known for its made-from-scratch menu. Owner and operator Damien Wyatt opened the business in 2019 on the south side of Savannah in Berwick, a busy shopping center off of Highway 17. In doing so he was following in the footsteps of his father, Daniel Cloutier, and leaning into his wealth of experience in the restaurant industry.

"Sports bars aren't new, but there is a stigma that you're just getting a bunch of frozen, fried food and washing it down with beer," Damien says. "I had a vision for taking two of my favorite things, good food and sports, and putting them together in a way where food is at the forefront."

With a menu based on his culinary journey—clam chowder and lobster rolls from New England; Cuban sandwiches from his time in Florida; and shrimp and grits, which he first ate in Georgia—Damien wanted as many dishes as possible to be scratch made, fresh, and delicious. All of the dressings and wing sauces are made in-house. "Our entrées aren't batched; we are making all our sautéed items to order," Damien says. "I smoke the pork for our Cubans and pulled-pork dishes, and our burgers and wings are never frozen." Bestsellers

The Draft Room includes a gaming area with pool tables and darts, as well as a comfortable covered patio. Visit their website for live music, trivia nights, and special community events.

Top left: The Draft Room at Berwick is designed with three distinct spaces: a cocktail bar, dining room, and gaming area. *Above left:* The Italian sandwich is served on ciabatta bread with ham, genoa salami, prosciutto, and provolone with a homemade Italian dressing. *Top right:* The steak flatbread features shaved rib eye, mushrooms, caramelized onions, roasted red peppers, mozzarella, and balsamic reduction, *Above right:* Owner Damien Wyatt (right) and Lead Cook Levar Washington (left) toast in the dining room. All photos courtesy of The Draft Room.

include the hot crab and artichoke dip, fish and chips, and of course, jumbo chicken wings, which are also available boneless. With 30 beers on draft and 20 TVs offering all the major sports packages and pay-per-view events, the atmosphere at The Draft Room is what Damien calls "a 2000s' *Cheers* of sorts."

Originally from Laconia, New Hampshire, Damien was exposed early to the service industry through his father's career. When he was 12 years old, his father was the food and beverage director for New Hampshire Motor Speedway, and Damien worked concessions. Through the years, his father owned several restaurants where Damien and his siblings often worked, including Molly MacPherson's Scottish Pub & Grill, a favorite downtown Savannah hangout for 18 years. Damien also worked as a culinary aid at a hospital, at a high-end golf course, and later for Darden Restaurants, the largest full-service restaurant group in the world. Each of these experiences taught him something new and helped to shape who he is today.

"The restaurant industry is not for the faint of heart," he says. "But I believe with hard work and effort, things can line up for anyone."

5730 Ogeechee Rd., Ste. 110
912-777-4768, tdrberwick.com

THE PARIS MARKET CAFÉ

A coffee shop that sparks wanderlust

Tucked inside the Paris Market and Brocante, one of Savannah's most elegant shops on lively Broughton Street where old meets new, is the Paris Market Café, a luxurious and cheerful Parisian-style coffee bar with colorful macarons peeking out of a tempting pastry case and the tantalizing aroma of fresh brewed coffee. Since 2004, hand-pulled espresso and locally made pastries have satisfied Savannahians and all who visit.

Founded by Paula and Taras Danyluk, the Paris Market opened in 2001, and the café followed in 2004. *Architectural Digest* named it "The Most Beautiful Coffee Shop in Georgia."

"We modeled our café after one of my favorite spots in Paris's sixth arrondissement—with simple yet delicious food and drink, comfortably chic seating, and lots of charm," says Paula. Drawn copper-colored curtains anchored by a one-of-a-kind chandelier frame a small wooden bar complete with four comfortable barstools at a picture window, perfect for people-watching. Tiny vases of fresh flowers serve as centerpieces on the marble bistro tables, and carefully curated vintage antiques give life to the very Instagrammable space. Plush velvet banquettes offer additional seating. Stop in for an afternoon pick-me-up in the midst of shopping, or enjoy a glass of champagne while sitting at the quaint row of sidewalk tables. In addition to coffee and cold brews, signature drinks, and loose-leaf

The Paris Market Café also features a kids' menu with Fruit & Fromage (seasonal fruit, cheese, and crackers), Milk & Cookies, and a crustless Petit Sandwich option.

Left: Pastry cases are filled with colorful macarons and homemade pastries from Auspicious Baking Co. *Right:* The Paris Market Café is a must-visit destination in downtown Savannah.

teas, the menu features French pastries such as gourmet pop tarts and pain au chocolat (chocolate bread), sandwiches, quiche, cookies, and ice cream delivered fresh from local bakeries daily.

Originally from New Orleans, Paula, a former speech pathologist, and her husband, Taras, an emergency physician, opened the Paris Market after being inspired by Marche aux Puces, the world's largest flea market in Saint-Ouen on the outskirts of Paris. A globetrotter, Paula personally selects all of the home goods and gifts, from scented candles, tote bags, wooden cutting boards, and linens to antiques from Europe and the Middle East. At the corner of Broughton and Whitaker Streets in downtown Savannah, the historic two-story Victorian building was originally constructed in 1874 as a grocery store. From the outside, you can't miss the unmistakable teal color highlighting the window trim and columns.

Influenced by their world travels, the Danyluks have created something truly special. With one walk through this unique shop and café, you'll be transported far away. "We strive to create a place where people can forget about everything and get lost in a world of beautiful, inspiring, and sometimes peculiar things," says Paula.

36 W Broughton St.
912-232-1500, theparismarket.com

MOLLY MCGUIRE'S

Unwind on island time

There's something about a good band and fried seafood that just hit the spot. Molly McGuire's is the kind of place where you can go after a day at the beach or on the boat to kick back and have a good time. Savannahians have been enjoying this locally owned island oasis since 2010 in its current location tucked away in the Wilmington Island Shopping Plaza, and prior to that dating back to 1979 when it was next door to Spanky's Pizza Galley & Saloon on River Street.

Part of the family of restaurants owned by Live Oak Restaurant Group, Molly McGuire's was opened by veteran Savannah restaurateur Ansley Williams, who got his start in the restaurant industry as a Georgia Tech student cooking hamburgers at the Bucket Shop in Underground Atlanta. With a menu featuring fresh local fare such as salads, sandwiches, fried seafood platters, and of course Spanky's chicken fingers and spuds, there is no shortage of variety. Items like blue crab dip, Ossabaw oysters and the Sapelo sampler with cheese sticks, fried pickles, and onion rings give a nod in their namesake to the barrier islands in the surrounding area and ingredients sourced on the Georgia coast. Molly's po'boys are served with your choice of fried seafood including shrimp, oysters, or fish. Try the fresh catch straight off the boat, or for a lighter dinner packed with flavor, the Thai grilled shrimp over rice and seasonal vegetables is a crowd-pleaser.

Whether you're enjoying a night out with friends and family, celebrating a birthday party, or watching the game during football season, Molly McGuire's has the space to accommodate. One of the focal points of the restaurant is its large covered gazebo made comfortable with plenty of ceiling fans in the summer and heaters in the winter. The wood-shingled roof contains Western red cedar

Left: A spread of Atlantic appetizers including nachos and teriyaki tuna bites, with bite-size pieces of grilled tuna glazed in teriyaki sauce. *Center:* The expansive outdoor gazebo is a comfortable spot to enjoy lunch or dinner with family and friends. *Top right:* The thai grilled shrimp is a popular choice among the locals. *Above right:* Red snapper is a fresh fish popular on the Georgia coast, available at Molly McGuire's grilled, fried, or blackened. All photos courtesy of Live Oak Restaurant Group.

in the ceiling and around the beams sourced from the docks of neighboring Hilton Head Island. Positioned over a peaceful lagoon surrounded by tropical vegetation, the gazebo offers flat-screen TVs for entertainment. Inside, hardwood floors and lively plants create a warm and welcoming respite from the Georgia heat.

A large dance floor can be hard to find in Savannah, but Molly McGuire's delivers. With 6,000 square feet of total dining space between the inside space and outdoor decks, including an outdoor bar, everyone has plenty of space to "eat, drink, and be Molly!"

216 Johnny Mercer Blvd., #1
912-898-0852, mollymcguiressavannah.com

On your first visit, Molly McGuire's can seem a bit out of the way. Look for it hidden behind a few other businesses in a large gravel parking area just off of Johnny Mercer Boulevard.

THE WYLD DOCK BAR

A waterfront eatery off the beaten path

If you're looking for a dining experience on the water, look no further than the Wyld, one of Savannah's only casual lunch and dinner waterfront eateries accessible by land or sea. Formerly known as Bonna Bella Yacht Club, the restaurant is owned and operated by Executive Chef Tony Seichrist and his business partner Brad Syfan, both from the Atlanta area. The seasonal menu is stripped down and laid back, offering only a handful of appetizers, entrées, and a few side dishes, but the setting and the view alone are worth a visit.

If you plan to arrive by vehicle, a large gravel parking area offers plenty of room. The Wyld is located at the end of Livingston Avenue with mostly outdoor seating and a few seats indoors. You place your order at a walk-up counter and find a table on the two roomy, pet-friendly porches at the water's edge. As you wander through the property, paved brick pathways guide the way through a grassy lawn, and big barrels of colorful flowers under the patio lights create a magical backdrop to the marsh grass and expansive sky. A garden brimming with bright blue containers of fresh herbs just outside the busy kitchen attracts butterflies and is a feast for the eyes. Adirondack chairs surrounding a large firepit and cornhole boards encourage good times. Toward the back of the restaurant are additional tables with large umbrellas and a well-stocked bar that faces the dock. On any given summer day, you can sit and watch the boats idling up slowly through the no-wake zone while egrets and wild herons fly overhead.

Chef Tony grew up hunting and fishing, and he learned to appreciate quality ingredients from his mother, who taught him to cook and garden. At 20 years old, he sought out the opportunity to train under Canadian-born chef and restaurateur Hugh Acheson. His love for the Lowcountry brought him to Cumberland Island,

Top left: Enjoy dining alfresco in one of the many seating areas among the gardens. *Above left:* Twice-cooked pork tacos are filled with onion, cilantro, fresh pineapple, and tomatoes and served with black beans. *Top right:* The shrimp roll is served on a buttered, toasted bun, with local shrimp, and a light dressing of mayonnaise, lemon juice, and chives. *Above right:* The Wyld is one of Savannah's popular waterfront restaurants welcoming hungry boaters to park at the dock.

where he served as the head chef at Greyfield Inn, and when the property where the Wyld sits today went on the market, the timing was right. The Wyld Dock Bar opened in April of 2015.

The Wyld is known for their local fish tacos served with a poblano aioli and rice and black beans; another popular dish is the crispy fried shrimp with french fries and cocktail sauce. They source their ingredients locally and know the local farmers and purveyors by name. Be sure to save room for dessert—the Key lime pie is highly recommended with a cold cocktail on the sea breeze.

2740 Livingston Ave.
912-692-1219, thewylddockbar.com

The Wyld Dock Bar does not accept cash or reservations.

DESPOSITO'S SEAFOOD

Isle of Armstrong nostalgia

Underneath the Thunderbolt bridge, just off of Highway 80 on the Wilmington River, is Desposito's Seafood, a storied Savannah institution with years of rich history that quietly closed its doors in 2020 but has opened again under new ownership, much to the delight and great anticipation of the locals. In what has been described as "a gritty seafood shack on the outskirts of Thunderbolt," Desposito's is now anything but gritty. After more than two years of renovations, the restaurant has been modernized and offers a menu that preserves the past and embraces the future.

To fully appreciate the new Desposito's, one must understand its legendary past. In 1965, at the age of 40, Carlo Desposito, an Italian dockworker, purchased what was the Walton family seafood market. He renamed the business Desposito's Seafood and continued to run it exactly as it had been: as a casual dive with simple seafood dishes such as boiled shrimp and blue crabs, deviled crab, and steamed oysters served over back issues of the *Savannah Morning News*. Nothing was fried, and there was no tartar sauce.

For more than 50 years, Desposito's was the place to go for a cold beer and to watch the NASCAR race on Sundays at the bar. With plenty of electric beer signs on the walls and a great jukebox, many Savannahians over the age of 60 will tell you, Desposito's was the place you went on a first date and the only place to be on a Saturday night. Though Carlo passed away in 1982, his wife, Walton Boone, ran Desposito's for years before her son David took ownership.

Today, Michelle Smith, a native of Ludowici, Georgia, and the new managing partner at Desposito's, welcomes the challenge of maintaining the memories of what Desposito's has meant to so many

Top left: A historic photo of Desposito's, circa 2008. *Above left:* Garlic lobster mac and cheese. *Top center:* Present-day Desposito's, after the renovation. *Above center:* Managers Jenny Butcher, Michelle Smith, and Shannon Nelson (left to right). *Right:* Managing Partner Michelle Smith with the crispy chicken sandwich and fries. All photos courtesy of Deposito's.

over the years while making changes. The newly renovated space features an open-air bar with seating for 50, serving eight beers on tap plus frozen drinks. There's a waterfront view, a stunning blue mural hand-painted by local artist Jimmy Butcher, and indoor seating. On the walls you'll find gestures to days gone by preserved in the relics and photographs. The menu now includes all 15 original dishes at Desposito's, like Lowcountry boil and crab legs, plus appetizers, shareable items, and fried seafood and tartar sauce, of course.

3501 Macceo Dr., Thunderbolt
912-897-9963, despositosseafood.com

Desposito's offers a takeout window and several picnic tables outside for those in a hurry. Live music creates an easygoing vibe on the river.

BELLA NAPOLI ITALIAN BISTRO

From the old country to the lowcountry

Bella Napoli (Beautiful Naples) Bistro is a little gem in downtown Savannah. The quaint and authentic Italian pizzeria opened in the fall of 2015 on State Street, and since then has stolen the hearts and appetites of all who enter. Stepping inside off the busy sidewalk is like stepping straight into Italy. Be instantly swept away by the aroma of simmering tomato sauce and the crooning of Luciano Pavarotii and Andrea Bocelli coming from the speakers. The dimly lit, romantic, intimate space evokes *Lady and the Tramp* vibes, making it the perfect date night destination.

Beneath a large green awning labeled "Chicken, Veal, Pasta, Panini, Wings, Seafood" with a single neon blue-and-red sign flashing "Open" in the window, Bella Napoli is next door to the iconic Bradley Lock and Key, the oldest locksmith shop in Georgia—in operation since 1883. Inside, you'll find candlelit red-and-white-checkered tablecloths, red walls with hand-painted murals of Pulcinella (a classical comedic character that originated in 17th-century Italy), along with messages such as "La Famiglia" (family) and "Ti Amo" (I love you) and rows of wine bottles lining a ledge near the ceiling. The professional waitstaff wear black and offer friendly, knowledgeable service.

For owner and operator Gary Langevin, creating ambiance was a top priority when he opened Bella Napoli Italian Bistro. The Naples, Italy,

Bella Napoli is perfect for small parties, seating no more than four guests per table. No split checks, please.

Left: Chef Gary Langevin (left) and staff members show their Italian pride in front of a spread of Bella Napoli's food and wine. *Right:* Bistro tables are available under the awning for dining alfresco. All photos courtesy of Emilie Kefalas for *South* magazine.

native is no stranger to the restaurant business. He is the founder of La Famiglia Restaurant Group, which operates more than 10 restaurants throughout the coastal Southeast, creating experiences for his guests and bringing others together through good food shared with friendship and affection—those same authentic values found in family.

Each meal begins with warm garlic bread served in a charming basket. On the seasonal menu, Bella Napoli is known for their expertly cooked pappardelle Bolognese with a homemade meat sauce, lobster ravioli, and the Parmesan wheel. Fresh-cooked pasta is tossed with butter or extra-virgin olive oil, swirled with cheese from a Parmesan wheel, and then topped with your choice of meat. Neapolitan cuisine showcases bright ingredients with a focus on simplicity, such as Bella Napoli's pizza margherita, which has just the right amount of spice. You'll also want to save room for dessert. Homemade Italian classics such as tiramisu, cannoli, and limoncello cake hit the spot.

Chef Gary's philosophy is simple: chi mangia bene vive bene (Those who eat well, live well)!

18 E State St.
912-495-5124, bellanapolibistro.com

DOTTIE'S MARKET

In praise of all grandmothers. In love of good food.

For Chef Chris Meenan and his wife, Ericka, opening Dottie's Market in the heart of Savannah's Historic District was their way of paying homage to Ericka's great-grandmother Dottie while simultaneously providing a gathering place for the community. Most accurately summed up as "A food destination for the nostalgia seeker and the story lover, where all are welcome and no one leaves hungry," Dottie's Market is like sensory overload in the very best kind of way.

Outside on the sidewalk, gorgeous bouquets of fresh flowers wrapped in brown paper hint of the charm inside. Upon entering, you'll take in the expansive space with vaulted ceilings and warm hardwood floors, filled with natural light from the large picture windows. There's a grab-and-go deli case, a marketplace filled with unique, handmade gifts and sundries made by local artisans, a full-service chef's counter with seating for a dozen and a view directly into the kitchen, and a coffee bar featuring Counter Culture's sustainably sourced freshly roasted beans. The fridge at Dottie's is also stocked with local brews and one-of-a-kind organic wines from lesser-known producers such as Breaking Bread's bubbly Pet Nat, a sparkling zinfandel from the Sonoma, California region.

Dottie's serves breakfast, lunch, and dinner, and you can choose to dine inside at a table, eat at the chef's counter, or take your treats to go. The sandwiches, salads, bowls, and desserts are perfect for a quick lunch break or leisurely picnic in one of Savannah's 22 squares,

Online ordering is also available.

Left: Dottie's Market is filled with cookbooks, local preserves, and hand-woven sweetgrass baskets. *Center:* Crispy chicken sandwich served with burrata, pesto, and oven-dried tomato on a brioche bun with a small cup of potato salad. *Right:* Co-owner Ericka Phillips trains an employee at the register.

and the ever-evolving menus are split into daytime and evening options. For breakfast, decadent pastries and hot, savory sandwiches are made in-house. The evening menu features shareables such as Dottie's Totties with homemade tater tots and pimento cheese alongside meat and fish selections with local fried fish and smoked prime rib. Soulful sides such as mac and cheese, creamed corn, and collard greens can be ordered à la carte. The flavorful food served on vintage china with polished silver utensils is a celebration of the Lowcountry, shining the spotlight on regional growers.

Like most Southern grandmothers, Dottie loved good food and viewed feeding others as a source of nourishment and an expression of love. Ericka inherited that quality, and it's evident in the caring hospitality she brings to the front-of-house, coupled with the refined dishes Chef Chris and his team deliver from the kitchen.

Though a young concept by Savannah standards, Dottie's Market is sure to become a neighborhood tradition.

207 W Broughton St.
912-921-9337, dottiesmarketsav.com

BROCHU'S FAMILY TRADITION

Wild beasts and friendly folks

A string of rowdy country songs sets the tone, from the Nitty Gritty Dirt Band's "Fishin' in the Dark" to David Allan Coe's "You Never Even Called Me by My Name," as big round wooden platters of whole chicken three ways—fried, charred, and as chicken salad—make their way out of the kitchen. The setting is a 1930s-era grocery store in Savannah's Starland District, now completely renovated with an industrial, open-concept feel. Brochu's Family Tradition serves "fried chicken and fancy seafood," or quality, casual food and drinks, and is the highly anticipated restaurant concept of James Beard Award–nominated Chef Andrew Brochu and his wife, Sophie.

The Brochus were previously in Chicago, where Chef Andrew worked for the Alinea Group at Roister, a one Michelin Star–rated restaurant with an impressive list of accolades such as Zagat's "The 7 Best Places to Eat Fried Chicken in Chicago," and *Esquire*'s "Best New Restaurants in America." During his time there, Chef Andrew created the restaurant's legendary fried chicken, and through an unforeseen set of circumstances he brought that same fried chicken to Savannah. Now about that chicken: you can order a whole or half chicken (the half is more than enough for two people), and it's served with gravy, sunchoke hot sauce, biscuits, and pickles. Also on

Brochu's is tucked away behind the storefronts on Bull Street; enter on 40th Street and look for the designated parking area across from the restaurant. Reservations are accepted and walk-ins welcome.

Left: Owners Andrew and Sophie Brochu. Photo courtesy of Robin Elise Maaya. *Center:* The golden brown biscuits, finished with sea salt. *Top right:* The whole chicken dinner features fried thighs, charred breast, chicken salad, gravy, chamomile spice, sunchoke hot sauce, biscuits, and pickles (left) and blueberry molasses pie with ice cream (right). *Above right:* The exterior of the restaurant and welcoming patio with ample outdoor seating.

the menu are inspired oyster preparations, such as Thai style, jerk spice jam, and roasted brown butter crunch.

In 2020, Chef Andrew had planned to open a restaurant in Chicago after departing Roister, but because of complications from the pandemic, things didn't go as planned. That's when the Brochus decided to move to Savannah, Sophie's hometown. Both Chef Andrew and Sophie have Southern roots, and opening their restaurant in Savannah turned out to be even more meaningful with a deep sense of family and home.

With a friendly pelican as a mascot, cheeky wallpaper in the restrooms, and old boat motors mounted on the wall, the fun-loving and lighthearted personality of the brand is evident on the menu and in the decor. A large patio with umbrella-covered picnic tables offers plenty of seating outside, along with a takeout window where you can place an order to go. The space is designed to be casual and welcoming, with two flat-screen TVs positioned on either side of a message board at the bar, often with classic movies like *Top Gun* on display.

Brochu's Family Tradition is serving up Southern hospitality and nostalgic food—get there soon.

2400 Bull St., Ste. 8
brochusfamilytradition.com

COMMON THREAD

Contemporary farm-to-table cooking

A six-partner team is behind the enlightening, refreshing dining experience at Common Thread, Savannah's newest renovated-mansion-turned-fine-dining-restaurant, with its namesake a cue to the relationship between them all and a singular mission to create community through food. With incredibly intentional and thoughtful detail from the fare to the atmosphere, Common Thread satisfies hunger, quenches thirst, and inspires curiosity.

The restaurant is located in Savannah's Thomas Square Neighborhood, once known as Millionaire's Row. Specifically, Common Thread occupies the historic Krouskoff House built in 1897 by businessman Solomon Krouskoff as a wedding present to his second wife, Matilda. In 2001 the home was sold to Albert L. Cobb Sr. and his wife, Lila, who owned an antiques business. The current owners acquired the home in 2018.

The fresh white walls and the contrasting gray wood-burning hearth create a calming, classy, undistracting, and tastefully decorated dining space where the often colorful food is the star of the show. On the main level are two large dining rooms, and upstairs there's a bar and lounge. Perhaps one of the most desirable tables is on the landing between floors, a Romeo and Juliet table for two reserved for special occasions. An original mural painted by a local art student is showcased on the walls.

For Chefs Brandon Carter and Joseph Harrison, the approach to the vegetable-heavy menu at Common Thread starts with what's available from the more than 30 regional farmers and producers from which they source ingredients. They draw inspiration from global cuisines, transforming Georgia-grown ingredients into bold, flavorful plates. Instead of traditional appetizers and entrées, the tasting menu

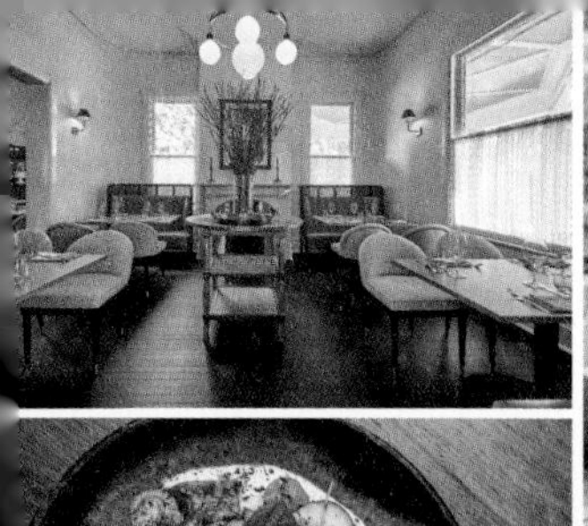

Top left: The large dining rooms on the main level include comfortable seating and muted decor. Photo courtesy of John Park. *Above left:* Tomato salad with benne seed, yogurt, cucumber, sumac, spring onion, and basil. Photo courtesy of SV Images. *Center:* Brandon Carter, executive chef and partner. Photo courtesy of Cameron Wilder. *Top right:* Sweet potato huancaína. Photo courtesy of SV Images. *Above right:* Bird of Paradise cocktail. Photo courtesy of Eastwood's Photography.

is grouped into four categories progressing from light to rich, and the knowledgeable waitstaff can offer guidance on how to navigate each one. As the seasons and availability of ingredients change, so will the menu. At the bar, expect produce-forward cocktails, wines from around the world, local brews, and European ciders. A Chef's Counter experience is offered each night, where guests interact with chefs as they craft a special four-course family-style menu with customized wine pairings.

Common Thread opened in January of 2021, making *Bon Appétit*'s coveted list of "50 Best New Restaurants of 2022." The magazine offered these observations: "Cold, plump local oysters practically jump out of their shells with the addition of pickled watermelon rind; beef tartare tastes fresher and grassier with a dose of lime and chile mirasol; a sunflower seed tahini brings out the earthy edges of summer tomatoes."

122 E 37th St.
912-944-7482, commonthreadsavannah.com

Common Thread is part of the same family behind FARM Bluffton in South Carolina's Lowcountry.

THE VAULT KITCHEN + MARKET

Asian fusion and Laotian cuisine

The unmistakable teal color ensures you won't overlook the Vault Kitchen + Market, a renovated Bank of America building turned industrial-chic eatery in the Starland District. For more than 50 years, the bank was a trusted local landmark in the community; today, in that same spirit, Rhino Hospitality, formerly known as Ele & the Chef Collection, strives to maintain that same sense of reliability, offering an Asian fusion, Laotian, and fresh seafood menu that delights and surprises the palate.

Ele Tran and her husband, chef Sean, together own Rhino Hospitality and are the power couple behind 11 Savannah restaurants. Ele's incredible story from refugee to restaurateur started when she was just an infant. When Ele was born, her family, fearing the communist government, fled Vietnam by boat, eventually landing in Indonesia for a year before an opportunity to immigrate to the US gave them a chance at a better life. After six months of English language courses, a refugee rescue service helped her entire family make it to America. From an early age her parents instilled in her a strong work ethic and entrepreneurial spirit. Later, Ele met Sean, originally from Laos, and together they found their way to Savannah, where in 2001 they opened their first restaurant. Nearly 23 years later, they have had immense success.

Inside the Vault Kitchen + Market, at what may be the best seat in the house, you can pull up a barstool to the kitchen at a large window facing the action. Relics of the former bank have been repurposed and displayed throughout the decor, including brightly painted safety deposit boxes, coins, and the former bank vault door leading

Top left: The Banker's shrimp tacos with grilled shrimp, mango, lettuce, pickled carrots and daikon, chipotle sauce, sesame seeds, cilantro, and kimchi dressing. *Above left:* Triple chocolate cake with fresh whipped cream and strawberries. *Top center:* Try a side of Parmesan roasted cauliflower. *Above center:* The Crying Tiger is gluten free and features grilled steak and Laos hot dipping sauce. *Right:* Author Rebekah Faulk Lingenfelser (left) and her aunt Susan Faulk Burford (right), visiting from Macon, Georgia, dine at the Vault Kitchen + Market in 2017.

into the Vault Room, a unique dining space that can be reserved for private parties. A large temperature-controlled patio with checkered flooring provides additional seating.

Menu highlights include classic sushi rolls and mains by land and sea, such as the miso salmon with sautéed shiitake mushrooms and charcoal chicken, turmeric spiced with Laotian hot dipping sauce. Sticky rice, the base of Laotian food, is served with many of the dishes.

"I am so grateful to be doing what I love and living this out here in the United States, as so many others have done after immigrating over the past centuries," Ele told the I AM TOURISM project. "The American dream came true for us with a lot of hard work and a fresh start. We are very grateful and remember this every single day."

They invite you to come and deposit some memories.

2112 Bull St.
912-201-1950, thevaultkitchen.com

Rhino Hospitality also own Little Duck Diner, Flying Monk Noodle Bar, and Chive Sea Bar & Lounge, among others, plus a French countryside interior design store. Visit rhinohospitalitygroup.com to check them out.

POE'S TAVERN

Edgar Allan Poe gastropub

In the former Savannah Fire Station just up the hill from the JW Marriott Savannah Plant Riverside District downtown is Poe's Tavern, a gastropub named for American writer and poet Edgar Allan Poe. Poe's specializes in ground-in-house hamburgers, fish tacos, sandwiches, and salads, and fans of grim and macabre literature will be delighted when they read the menu and recognize some of their favorite stories honored, such as the Beef Raven or Chicken Black Cat. Eerily beautiful Savannah, known as one of the most haunted places in Georgia, is a fitting location for this Edgar Allan Poe–themed restaurant. It's been open for just over a year now and is the only one of its kind in the state.

Poe's is known for its hand-cut fries, moody ambiance, and friendly service, and the menu features popular selections such as Edgar's nachos with Edgar's drunken chili, bacon cheese fries, and half-pound burgers cooked to order. Several of the menu items are vegetarian, including vegan and gluten-free options. At the bar, 24 draft beers with an emphasis on high-quality regional and local selections are up for grabs.

An excerpt from the menu tells the story of Poe's life and impact:

> *Much like his work, the life of Edgar Allan Poe was short, tragic, and shrouded in mystery. Best known as the author of the popular poem "The Raven," Poe is credited with creating the detective and horror story genres. After a brief stint at the University of Virginia, Poe enlisted in the army under the pseudonym Edgar Allan Perry,*

Poe's Tavern also has locations in Sullivan's Island, South Carolina; Atlantic Beach, Florida; and Wrightsville Beach, North Carolina.

Left: The Beef Black Cat with grilled onions, Edgar's drunken chili, applewood bacon, and pimento cheese. *Center:* Poe's Tavern, along with JTVS Builders Inc., earned first place for the Poe's Project renovation from the Association of General Contractors Build Georgia Awards. *Top right:* Throughout the restaurant, framed photos and posters of Poe and his work fill the light-green-painted walls. *Above right:* The Beef Amontillado is served with fresh toppings such as pico de gallo, guacamole, and jalapeño jack cheese. All photos courtesy of Poe's Tavern.

and was stationed at Fort Moultrie at the western end of Sullivan's Island, SC, for thirteen months beginning Nov. 18, 1827. His time on the island inspired "The Gold Bug," a story about a mystical beetle that led to buried treasure. He died alone, impoverished, and inebriated at the age of 40 amid conflicting accounts of his demise, yet left an indelible legacy on American literature.

Poe was one of the first well-known American writers to earn a living through writing alone, but it wasn't always much of a living. Near the entrance, a haunting painted portrait of Poe is etched into the exposed brick, and down the hallway toward the restrooms is a dimly lit library of books. On the wall above a U-shaped booth nook is painted a famous quote from Poe: "Fill with mingled cream and amber, I will drain that glass again. Such hilarious visions clamber through the chamber of my brain. What care I how time advances? I am drinking ale today."

7 Martin Luther King Jr. Blvd.
912-561-7637, poestavern.com

LULU'S CHOCOLATE BAR

Desserts and martinis for days

"When a baker and a bartender combine their strengths to pursue a creative vision, a beautiful thing happens," says Janine Finn, co-owner of Lulu's Chocolate Bar. In 2007, she and Rebecca Radovich did exactly that, and their efforts have paid off. Voted best desserts in Savannah for 16 years in a row by local media (that's every year they've been open), Lulu's Chocolate Bar has solidified its place in the Hostess City of the South, with decadent desserts and an array of specialty drinks and martinis. Lulu's is the perfect spot to celebrate a birthday or anniversary, or to grab a nightcap after dinner downtown. Their seasonal menu and glamorous atmosphere promise a good time, all while being totally on trend and social media friendly.

Baked fresh every morning, the made-from-scratch cakes, pies, cheesecakes, tortes, brownies, and chocolate-covered strawberries fill a large pastry case—the first thing you see when you walk through the door. "For desserts in general, this is the place to come," said Mike Grompper, general manager. Lulu's signature Strawberry Suspension Cake is one of their most popular desserts, with two layers of rum-brushed chocolate cake and a center of mascarpone cheese with strawberries suspended inside. The white chocolate–chocolate chip cheesecake served with a white chocolate raspberry swirl is another crowd-pleaser.

Half bar, half bakery, Lulu's offers a full bar with 19 martini variations. "Our Lulutini is like a whole bunch of chocolate exploding in your mouth, which is fantastic," Mike says. Featuring Van Gogh Dutch Chocolate Vodka and Lulu's very own sipping chocolate, the Lulutini is a must-try.

With a background as a business manager and yacht stewardess, Janine focuses more on the bar side of the business, while Rebecca, who formerly owned a catering business, oversees the desserts. Lulu's is

Top left: Janine Finn (left) and Rebecca Radovich (right), owners. Photo courtesy of Lulu's Chocolate Bar. *Above left:* The Praline pecan pie with a shortbread crust is a fan favorite. Photo courtesy of Lulu's Chocolate Bar. *Top right:* A slice of chocolate chip big cookie with ice cream. Photo courtesy of Lulu's Chocolate Bar. *Above right:* Lulu's Chocolate Bar also offers outdoor seating on the sidewalk.

located in the heart of downtown on the main thoroughfare of Martin Luther King Jr. Boulevard; you can't miss the bright pink logo of Lulu's on the front window of the business. And just who is Lulu? "You know, everybody embodies Lulu," says Mike. "Whether it's the dessert or the drink side. It's a fictional character, but we all kind of embody Lulu."

When the sun goes down, so does lighting inside of Lulu's romantic space with its gold accents and hot-pink bar.

"We have been overwhelmed by the positive feedback, and with all the friends we have made working at the restaurant," says Janine. "We really love what we do. Come and enjoy our passion."

42 Martin Luther King Jr. Blvd.
4700 Hwy. 80, Ste. E
912-480-4564, luluschocolatebar.com

Lulu's Chocolate Bar does not accept reservations. On-street parking is available, or you can find a spot in a nearby parking garage downtown.

THE WRIGHT SQUARE BISTRO

Fine food. Wine. Chocolates.

For nearly 20 years, the Wright Square Cafe operated at 21 York Street, until Michael Higgins and Tod Whitaker purchased the space in June of 2021. The partners rebranded the restaurant, changing its name to the Wright Square Bistro, creating a casual-gourmet bistro and pantry with a focus on seasonal, freshly prepared food with a distinctly Southern flair. They offer one of the largest selections of gourmet chocolates in the South, sourced as far as Paris, and even Belgium marzipan.

Tod had not always dreamed of opening his own café, but life has its surprises. "COVID happened; things happened and this became available, and it's been fun," he says. Born and raised in North Carolina, Tod moved to New York City on a full scholarship to attend Parsons School of Design for art. "I ended up waiting tables at this little company called Smith Barney, which turned into Citigroup," he says. He became their executive vice president of food service for 25 years. In 2014, he moved to Savannah and worked as the general manager for Goose Feathers Cafe, a European-style café and bakery just around the corner from what is now the Wright Square Bistro.

"Ninety-five percent of everything we have is done in Savannah," he says. "Even our sodas are Southern based." Famous for their meat loaf sandwich, served with cheddar cheese and special sauce

South magazine named the Wright Square Bistro to its list of "the South's Greatest Places of 2023," calling it "everything you'd expect from a cozy corner bistro, and then some."

Left: Signature bottled items such as hot pickled okra fill the shelves inside. *Center:* Southern Waldorf Salad with grilled seasonal fruit and pecan-crusted goat cheese. Photo courtesy of the Wright Square Bistro. *Right:* Visit the Wright Square Bistro for lunch or a pick up something to go.

on country bread, the bistro offers a mouthwatering selection of soups; salads; and sides, such as beer-battered onion rings, red potato salad, and mac and cheese. For the wide variety of desserts, Tod and Michael partner with other Savannah-based businesses. "Our desserts are all made by three ladies here in town: Abby and Sophie, who run Wicked Cakes," he says. "[And] Ms. Donna, with Donna's Delights, does my pound cake and my pecan pie." They serve Georgia beers and offer wines (by the glass or bottle) that center on boutique and organic vineyards rarely found elsewhere. RC Cola and A&W Root Beer are nostalgic beverage choices. Savannah Coffee Roasters provides the coffee beans, and Auspicious Baking Co. (page 50) supplies the croissants, breads, and pastries.

With its mustard-colored window trim and burgundy doors, the Wright Square Bistro offers sidewalk seating outside, even accommodating your furry friends with ceramic bowls of cold water. The restaurant is split into two rooms, with one side including a walk-up counter with a tempting case of chocolates, and the other a large dining room with warm hardwood floors and small vases of fresh flowers on every table.

21 W York St.
912-238-1150, wrightsquarebistro.com

SIX PENCE PUB

Fine ale. Fine food.

Marked by a bright red British telephone booth in the historic district of Savannah, Six Pence Pub sits at the corner of Bull Street and West Perry Lane and has been called the most authentic English pub in Georgia, perhaps for its charming plating and convivial atmosphere. Founded in 1999, the restaurant serves traditional American and British comfort food and has a variety of seasonal and craft beers on tap. It's the perfect spot to relax with friends over a pint or to enjoy a meal late into the night.

Union Jack flags hang just beneath the Magnolia and Spanish moss–covered oak trees on the sidewalk, and the exterior of tan brick with green and gold paint flanked by lantern lights on either side of the restaurant's nameplate beckons travelers from near and far. A shadow box containing the menu is mounted outside, informing visitors of the starters, public house offerings, and daily specials, such as the prime rib sandwich with au jus and homemade soups including tomato basil and French onion. On the menu you'll find loaded bangers as a starter, with English-style Cumberland sausage—a pork sausage that originated in the historic county of Cumberland, England—often very long and served rolled in a coil, stuffed with mashed potato, bacon, and cheddar cheese. Hearty, stick-to-your-ribs entrées such as shepherd's pie, bangers and mash, and tender pot roast are served with a house salad or the vegetable of the day to round out the meal. Warm bowls of soup are placed atop white lace doilies for a delightful presentation.

At the bar, a row of character jugs, ceramic statues featuring familiar faces of the British Parliament and British royal family and made popular by the Staffordshire potters in the 1760s, decorate the space. Etele K., an excited Yelp reviewer, commented upon sight

Top left: Outdoor seating is perfect for people watching on the sidewalk. *Above left:* The soup and half sandwich combo is available as lighter fare. *Top right:* Shepherd's pie with a salad of crisp greens. *Above right:* Inside the dining room, a server attends to guests.

of them, "Toby jugs! The Queen having a drink with us!" Framed photographs of a young Queen Elizabeth hang on the wall. A large selection of specialty coffees, single-malt scotch, premium bourbons, cognac, and port are available. In the dining area, round tables make for great conversation, while warm wood tones, red carpet, and plaid wallpaper create a welcoming atmosphere.

Prior to Six Pence Pub, the building was Wally's Sixpence, a pub for 40 years in Savannah run by Wally and Doris, a London couple who understood how to make British expatriates and locals feel right at home. Family owned, Six Pence Pub continues that tradition today.

245 Bull St.
912-233-3151, sixpencepub.com

Six Pence Pub opened a second location in 2001 in Blowing Rock, North Carolina. *Condé Nast Traveler* named the original location in Savannah one of the "14 Best Bars" to visit.

JAZZ'D TAPAS BAR

A sultry underground hot spot

English poet Rupert Brooke said, "Cities, like cats, will reveal themselves at night." At the corner of Barnard and Broughton Streets, located underground beneath Gap Inc., Jazz'd Tapas Bar has been a chic part of the Hostess City's nightlife since 2003; it's unlike anything else in Savannah. The go-to place to gather for craft cocktails, live music, and tapas, the restaurant is described as an Americanized version of centuries-old Spanish tradition. *Cosmopolitan* magazine called it one of the "Sexiest places in the world—a must do." You may think the name only refers to the style of music, but it's better to think of it more as a state of mind.

Featuring an elevated menu, Jazz'd offers more than 30 tapas, slightly larger than appetizers and designed so you can order multiple plates and share them. There are several gluten-free and vegetarian options, and you'll also find savory soups and fresh salads on the menu. Lamb chops with garlic and rosemary and the firecracker shrimp spring rolls with flash-fried, basil-wrapped shrimp and a spicy chili glaze are crowd-pleasers. The tapas for two, a great way to tour the menu, features your choice of soup or salad with four tapas, two desserts, and a soft drink or coffee for a fixed price.

A staircase leads you down into the expansive, swanky space, where you'll find a sleek serpentine bar, modern lighting, and an industrial-chic scene. Live music from many genres including blues, swing, jazz, classic rock, pop, and Americana is offered several nights

Reservations are accepted for large parties only. Must be 18 or older to enter.

Top: Sip one of the properly garnished, mixologist-created craft cocktails. *Above left:* The sleek bar and moody dining area inside Jazz'd Tapas Bar. *Above right:* Take the staircase below street level straight into sophisticated nightlife. All photos courtesy of Jazz'd Tapas Bar.

a week. Classical vocals in the style of Frank Sinatra and Savannah's own Johnny Mercer set the tone for an evening to dance the night away. Creative libations such as Bessie's Empress with Empress gin, cucumber shrub, and lemon, or the Safe Passage featuring Scotch whiskey, honey ginger syrup, and candied ginger will excite the palate. Try a specialty martini or a glass of Veuve Clicquot, a famous French champagne.

A comfortable lounge area is available while you wait for a table, including attentive service. Visit for a girls night out or a date night on the town. The clientele is well dressed and ready for a good time. It's an upscale place to let your hair down.

52 Barnard St.
912-236-7777, jazzdtapasbar.com

RACHAEL'S RESTAURANT & BAR

Sports. Food. Fun.

On the south side of Savannah everyone knows where to go to watch the game, order a pizza, and enjoy drinks with friends. It's Rachael's Restaurant & Bar, the hidden jewel of Georgetown. With a 17-inch TV wall, the largest in Savannah, and a state-of-the-art sound system, the neighborhood sports bar has an expansive outdoor patio and bar, pool tables inside, and a great sense of humor displayed in the "Dad Joke of Day" on a sign near the entrance.

Established in 2011, the former seafood restaurant is owned by Rachael Aldinger and her husband, Darin, originally from Philadelphia. With a mission to create an entertaining and enjoyable dining and social experience worthy of sharing with the community, they specialize in American-style, casual dining. "We take pride in every drink and dish we put before our guests," says Rachael. "All food is cooked to order and made fresh from local ingredients, whenever possible." The menu features a variety of specialty salads, sandwiches, grass-fed burgers, and entrées such as the Big as a House Quesadilla—two huge tortillas filled with chicken, bacon, and cheese. The Mom's Award Winning Pizza, named in honor of Rachael's mom, is hand-tossed, with a soft yet crispy dough spread with pesto and topped with cheese, chicken, and bacon. Order a side of ranch dressing along with it for dipping the crust.

On the lighter side, the Cali Chicken Wrap has great flavors—marinated, grilled chicken breast is wrapped with Swiss cheese, avocado, applewood bacon, and jalapeño aioli. Darin's Philly Cheesesteak comes straight from the family kitchen with shaved rib eye, grilled onions, and melted aged provolone on Amoroso rolls,

Top left: Rachael's Restaurant & Bar has a large parking area free of charge. *Above left:* A side Caesar salad with Caesar dressing. *Top right:* Mom's Award Winning Pizza. *Above right:* The view inside the primary dining room.

shipped directly from Philly. Since 1904, Amoroso's Baking Company and its authentic Italian hearth-baked rolls have been the foundation for legendary Philly cheesesteaks, hoagies, and sandwiches.

The later in the evening it gets, the more lively the clientele becomes. Wooden tables fill the center of the dining room with booths along the weathered tin walls. Electric beer signs, flags promoting the Philadelphia Eagles, and a cardboard cutout of Conor McGregor, an Irish professional mixed martial artist, decorate the restaurant. More than 15 HDTVs are on display. "We offer some of the best sports and entertainment technology in the region," says Rachael.

Rachael's Restaurant & Bar is open for lunch and dinner.

1190 King George Blvd.
912-920-7772

After 9 p.m., Rachael's Restaurant & Bar is most suitable for an adult audience.

RANCHO ALEGRE CUBAN RESTAURANT

Cuban and Caribbean cuisine with Latin flair

If you're looking for a lively night out with flavorful food, friendly service, and all the verve of the Latino community, look no further than Rancho Alegre Cuban Restaurant. Rancho Alegre, or "Happy Ranch" as it translates, is a local favorite owned by the father-daughter team of Melody Rodriguez and Juan Manuel Rodriguez, both natives of Venezuela. The Cuban eatery and bar is famous for its traditional dishes and beverages, which they've been sharing with Savannah for nearly 25 years.

Located in what used to be the Metro Coffee House on Martin Luther King Jr. Boulevard at the corner of Jones Street, the family-owned restaurant specializes in Cuban food, but also showcases popular dishes from Puerto Rico, Colombia, and Venezuela. The bestseller is the Plato Mixto, or mixed plate, which offers a tour of Cuba. The dish features shredded beef and roasted pork and chicken with mojo sauce along with rice, beans, and sweet plantains. Juan's most treasured recipe is the Paella Valenciana, featuring chicken, shrimp, clams, mussels, calamari, and grouper filets slowly cooked in a rice base with fish stock, white wine, saffron, and olive oil. "We pride ourselves on making food in small batches, so that the flavors and condiments are enjoyed," says Melody. Authentic sides such as yuca (the root of the cassava plant), and tostones (fried green plantains) are available with lunch or dinner, along

Reservations are encouraged during weekend nights. On-street parking is available, with a small parking area behind the restaurant.

Left: Fried red snapper dressed with fresh lime and tomatoes. Photo courtesy of Rancho Alegre. *Center:* Refreshing mojito. Photo courtesy of Kat Arntzen. *Top right:* Co-owner Juan M. Rodriguez in his "Best Cuban North of Miami and Tampa" T-shirt, celebrating the restaurant's 21st anniversary. Photo courtesy of Somi Studios. *Above right:* The Plato Mixto features a portion of each of the bestsellers: roasted chicken, lechón asado, and ropa vieja. Photo courtesy of Rancho Alegre.

with popular appetizers and soups such as empanadas de carne (stuffed beef pie), and homemade sopa de pollo (chicken soup). Wash it all down with an icy batido (milkshake) with tropical fruits, a well-known Latin American drink, or a cocktail from Rancho Alegre's homemade mojitos, sangria, and caipirinha.

Inside the expansive restaurant with its bright yellow walls are colorful tile accents, creating an inviting ambiance. Horns and trumpets adorn the walls above the stage where live bands play jazz music with a Latin vibe on the weekends. Rancho Alegre is an excellent choice if you are dining out with a large party, and the menu offers something for every diet, with ample vegan and vegetarian options. Emily G. from Jacksonville, Florida, dined at Rancho Alegre with a group of girlfriends and they were impressed. She left a Yelp review saying, "If you are in Savannah, don't walk, run to this amazing restaurant. As soon as you walk in, you are comforted by delicious smells, entertaining music and excellent service."

With Savannah's open-container policy, Rancho Alegre's frozen cocktails are a popular to-go option for sipping in the city's historic downtown area.

402 Martin Luther King Jr. Blvd.
912-292-1656, ranchoalegrecuban.com

BULL STREET TACO

For the simple joy of a great taco

For six years, Bull Street Taco has been a mainstay of the Starland District neighborhood, gaining popularity with tourists and locals with each passing year. Within walking distance of Forsyth Park, one of Savannah's iconic attractions, the owners have built a reputation for organic, handmade corn and flour tortillas, fresh-squeezed house margaritas, and "Tacos for a Cause" Tuesdays.

Recently, to keep up with the demand for business, the restaurant acquired the property next door—a former barbershop—and closed for a little more than two weeks to complete a renovation. With the additional 1,000 square feet of space, they gained a new full bar, an additional restroom, and an expanded kitchen, allowing more room for food preparation and storage. The aesthetic is Baja California, with framed images of surfboards and palm trees on the exposed brick walls, lime-green barstools, and a menu as diverse and eclectic as its clientele.

The tortillas are sourced from Mitla Tortilla Company, a Savannah-based wholesale manufacturer that specializes in making certified USDA organic flour and corn tortillas with no preservatives. Categorized into "before tacos," "instead of tacos," and "after tacos," the menu indicates that onions, jalapeños, and cilantro come on just about everything. The queso fundido is a must-try appetizer, made with roasted poblano, chorizo sausage, and tomatoes, and served with warm, seasoned, and crispy tortilla chips. Creative taco flavors abound, from Baja fish with tempura fried cod and tomatillo buttermilk crema to red chili tempura cauliflower served with chiles and basil crema on a corn tortilla. The street taco combo is a great way to enjoy a variety of flavors, and it comes with one side. Choose from chancho beans, cilantro basmati rice, or agave dijon slaw to name a few.

Top left: A large, covered, and pet-friendly patio is available for outdoor dining. *Above left:* Queso fundido with tortilla chips. *Right:* The Smoke and Fire Margarita comes highly recommended.

Bull Street is owned by John Massey and his wife, Sharon. John grew up in the restaurant industry and was an executive chef at other notable Savannah restaurants before opening his own place. He understands what it's like to work on major holidays, such as Thanksgiving and Christmas, and he strives to create a culture for his staff where time with friends and family is honored. Bull Street Taco closes every Sunday, on all the major holidays, and for a week in the summer typically coinciding with the Fourth of July—an idea almost unheard of in the restaurant business. It is evident the owners have a heart for the food and beverage community, giving back and supporting local.

1608 Bull St.
912-349-6931, bullstreettaco.com

During the pandemic, Bull Street Taco donated 400 burritos in a span of three hours to food and beverage workers, as a thank-you for supporting the restaurant during shutdowns. Every Tuesday the restaurant supports a local nonprofit to help bring the community together.

RHETT

Accessible coastal cuisine

Inside the Alida Hotel Savannah, a riverfront boutique hotel, is Rhett, the Alida's signature River Street restaurant. Offering coastal cuisine that celebrates the bounty of the Lowcountry, Executive Chef Alex Bollinger and his team serve brunch and dinner seven days a week in an upscale, refined atmosphere complete with a raw bar.

A native of San Francisco's East Bay, Chef Alex graduated from the Culinary Institute of America and moved to New York to work at Aureole, Chef Charlie Palmer's flagship restaurant, which has earned 13 Michelin Stars and two James Beard Awards. During his culinary career, Alex has worked alongside many notable chefs, including Eric Ziebold, previous chef de cuisine at the famed French Laundry, and celebrity chef and television host Tyler Florence. Today he brings his flourish and culinary style, heavily reliant on the seasonal and regional produce from the land and sea, to the Hostess City.

With brunch, dinner, and dessert menus to choose from, the wide variety of flavors is enticing and exciting. Many restaurants serve brunch on the weekends, but at the Rhett, you can order brunch any time before 2 p.m. daily. House favorites include bananas Foster French toast, shrimp and grits, chicken and waffles, and buttermilk biscuits and gravy with sausage country gravy and two eggs any style. Healthy options are also available, such as the coconut acai bowl and avocado toast. The dinner menu is categorized into selections from the raw bar, small plates, soups and salads, mains, and sides. Classic Lowcountry dishes including she-crab soup, blue crab cake, and roasted sea scallops proudly represent the Georgia coastal region. The mushroom tartine is a popular small plate with assorted roasted mushrooms, fresh herbs, and Boursin cheese on focaccia finished with parmesan and garlic

Top left: Alex Bollinger, executive chef at the Alida. *Above left:* Roasted sea scallops. *Center:* Brunch is served seven days a week. *Top right:* Libations include plenty of specialty cocktails, draft and canned beer, wine and nonalcoholic selections. *Above right:* Mushroom tartine with assorted roasted mushrooms, fresh herbs, and Boursin cheese. All photos courtesy of Rhett.

oil. For dessert, you'll recognize familiar Southern favorites such as banana pudding, a sweet Georgia brown sundae, cardamom cinnamon beignets, and oatmeal chocolate chip cookies.

In addition to brunch and dinner, Rhett offers "Sparkling Hour," a happy hour of sorts complete with the chef's selection of shareable bites paired with a crisp sparkling wine. On select days, local musicians provide live entertainment to accompany this event in the lounge or bar area.

Located directly across the street from the JW Marriott Savannah Plant Riverside District, Rhett is within walking distance of many shops and attractions in the entertainment district. An exquisite choice for a romantic date night or special outing with friends and family, Rhett delivers on service, ambiance, and taste.

412 Williamson St.
912-715-7000, ext. 4575, diningwithrhett.com

Valet parking is available. The Alida is also home to the Lost Square, an inviting rooftop bar with warm fireplaces and stunning panoramas of the riverfront.

SHUK MEDITERRANEAN

Eastern Mediterranean cuisine

In the former Foundery Coffee Pub in Savannah's Victorian District is one of the city's most fresh and interesting dining options: Shuk Mediterranean, a counter service–focused restaurant with a full bar and espresso café. The menu is inspired by owner Alexis Levin's Israeli heritage and the Eastern Mediterranean, and the one-of-a-kind, calming indoor and outdoor design concept is reason enough to visit.

Originally from Boston with family roots in Israel, Alexis moved to Savannah after college seeking a place to put down roots. After years of working in the food and beverage industry, she was inspired to start a concept of her own. She had worked in Savannah for four years before purchasing her current space, and she realized there was a lack of Mediterranean cuisine in the area. Her dad is Israeli, and she believed Savannah's growing community and ever-changing landscape of people would accept the flavors she wanted to bring to the table. After a complete design overhaul and renovation, Shuk Mediterranean opened in November of 2022.

"A shuk is an open-air market in Israel where you can find a little bit of everything," says Jess Spivey, service manager. "It's very eclectic." In Israel and other Middle Eastern countries, a shuk is a lively convergence of communities where everything from fresh fruits and vegetables, baked goods, and sweets, to art and antiques, homeware, and clothing are available. In that same spirit, the variety of foods offered and a melting pot of cultures is the idea behind the restaurant concept.

"Alexis works together with the chef and kitchen team to curate a menu that highlights not only Israeli foods but Syrian cuisine and cuisine from Turkey, Egypt, and Morocco," says Jess. "So many different places are blended together in a way that is still approachable for people who may not have experienced Mediterranean food before."

Left: A variety of chilled mezze, including Israeli salad, za'atar olives, hummus, house-marinated feta, and more. *Center:* The interior of the restaurant features cheerful colors and lively paintings. *Right:* Hummus #1 features spiced chickpeas, olive oil, smoked paprika, and parsley. Hummus #2 features chicken shawarma, harissa honey, and crispy sumac onions. All photos courtesy of Eastwoods Photography.

The menu features fresh, honest, and creative fare, with mainstays such as hummus, falafel, pita sandwiches, small plates, and salads. The chicken shawarma is a popular dish that you can order in a pita or a bowl with couscous, rice, or mixed greens. Topped with hummus, Israeli salad, and pickled cabbage, each dish is colorful and packed with flavor. Dips such as whipped feta with crushed pistachios and pomegranate honey are served with a pita and crudite.

Shuk Mediterranean is open for lunch, dinner, and brunch. As they say, "At Shuk, there are no strangers, just friends we haven't met yet!"

1313 Habersham St.
912-335-4340, shuksavannah.com

The climate-controlled outdoor patio features a flowing wall fountain designed with beautiful mosaic tiles and a full bar with ample seating. Live entertainment is often scheduled.

FRIENDSHIP COFFEE COMPANY

Good friends deserve great coffee

In a charming little spot tucked away in a strip mall off of Johnny Mercer Boulevard on Wilmington Island is Friendship Coffee Company, which began as a wholesale distributor in 2013. A woman-owned small business belonging to Libby Miller and Gay Fortson, the company expanded into a full coffee shop in 2016 when Hurricane Matthew hit Savannah and many were without power. Gay and Libby opened their doors—one of the few places with electricity at the time—to feed their neighbors and have never looked back.

Breakfast and lunch are served all day, and the homegrown recipes are made from scratch, featuring a variety of breakfast burritos, salads, and sandwiches. Popular selections such as the bacon, egg, and cheese biscuit; avocado toast; and apple crumb bread delight the palate, and the My Friend's Burger is a Black Angus burger that comes piled high with a juicy fried egg, cheddar cheese, bacon, lettuce, tomato, and griddled onions. The French onion soup is made with sweet Vidalia onions and topped with crusty French bread toasted to perfection with Swiss cheese.

Inside, the atmosphere has been described as akin to the coffee shop on the popular American sitcom *Friends*. With chalkboard menus, a stage for live entertainment, and a cozy corner including a couch and love seat, there's not a bad seat in the house. Books and

Follow Friendship Coffee Company on social media to catch one of their popular comedy shows or open-mic nights.

Left: Build your own bagel from an assortment of meats, cheeses, and veggies on the breakfast menu. *Center:* Avocado toast with fresh-baked romano cheese bread, smashed avocado, shaved radish, sliced cherry tomato, microgreens, and balsamic reduction. *Right:* Soak up the sunshine and take a seat on the sidewalk.

board games are also made available to encourage hanging out and making new friends. Shelves are filled with a variety of packaged goods from local vendors and artisans in the Savannah area.

In addition to the warm and friendly service, the coffee is the star of the show. Premium Arabica Brazil coffee beans from South America are roasted in small batches to order. Grown at high elevations with plenty of natural rainfall, the coffee beans are handpicked at the ripest stage of the fruit and double-sorted by hand to ensure freshness and quality. The cold-brew coffee is brewed and bottled by hand in Savannah and is 65 percent less acidic than heat-brewed coffee, producing a smooth cup for those who are typically unable to drink coffee products. Gay and Libby only source from fair-trade farms across the globe.

For those visiting Tybee Island, Friendship Coffee Company is a short jaunt for anyone who may not want to make the drive to Savannah. The clientele is a mix of creatives working remotely, sports groups, church groups, and moms.

"It's all about community," Gay told the *Savannah Morning News*. "It's more than just our love of coffee. This is a place where people come in and relax."

205 Johnny Mercer Blvd., Ste. 1
912-335-7634, friendshipcoffeeco.com

STARLAND CAFÉ

Quaint lunch fare

Off the beaten path in a residential neighborhood is the Starland Café, a casual lunch spot in a simple blue Victorian home with a double-decker porch, a periwinkle fence, and on-street parking. Offering indoor dining downstairs and porch and patio dining outside, the unique café serves panini sandwiches, homemade soups, and fresh salads made with local produce and organic ingredients. For more than 20 years, Starland Café has served the locals, and naturally, as the Starland District has grown, so has the café's customer base.

Owner and chef Michael Pritchard got his start in the restaurant industry washing dishes at a restaurant on Hilton Head Island. He later moved to Savannah, where he managed The Olde Pink House at just 23 years old. Before opening Starland Café, he previously owned two other food establishments in Savannah: Good Eats Restaurant and Cafe Zeum within the Jepson Center for the Arts. Chef and general manager Drew Wren joined the team nearly 13 years ago, and together they have made a successful go at lunchtime service and catering. The café offers two menus, with one dedicated to lunch offerings and the other a market menu focused on the catering side of the business. The market menu features large platters and chilled items by the pint, quart, or bottle, such as red grape chicken salad or Italian marinara sauce. These items are perfect for the family refrigerator, taking to parties, or as a gift to a friend or neighbor.

On the lunch menu, the Kitchen Sink Salad is one of the bestsellers, with a house-made buttermilk dressing, grilled asparagus, marinated artichokes, and crunchy rice noodles for texture. Creative paninis, or grilled sandwiches, such as the Cuban with sliced cumin-roasted pork tenderloin, ham, swiss cheese, and the café's own herb sauce inspire curiosity, while the CBG panini with grilled chicken

Left: Starland Café blends into the residential street—look for the periwinkle picket fence and matching front door to find it. *Top right:* The Mediterranean panini with grilled chicken salad, red grapes, marinated artichokes, fresh tomato, feta cheese, and basil pesto. *Above right:* The Starzanella Salad features herb vinaigrette, ciabatta croutons, feta cheese, roasted brussels sprouts, olives, peppers, sundried tomato, and red onion. All photos courtesy of Starland Café.

breast, thick bacon, caramelized onions, and house guacamole is an explosion of flavor. All the sandwiches are served with chips, and the soups, stews, and chili specials vary daily. Try the Tomato Thai, the famous house soup, served with stir-fried squash, thai seasoning, and coconut milk. A wide selection of plant-based, vegan, and gluten, free options are available, such as the Starzanella Salad with roasted brussels sprouts and sun-dried tomatoes.

Starland Café does not accept reservations and welcomes customers on a first-come, first-served basis.

11 E 41st St.
912-443-9355, thestarlandcafe.com

A charming short-term vacation rental with a view of the colorful homes on the block is located above the Starland Café. Known as "Sunny Apartment in Starland," it can be found on Airbnb and other travel sites.

ALLIGATOR SOUL

Upscale. Unpretentious. Unique.

Descend the secret staircase to deliciousness. In one of Savannah's most unique fine-dining destinations, you'll exit busy Barnard Street and step into a modern underground setting and a world of gracious hospitality—but don't blink or you'll miss it. Alligator Soul, founded in March of 2003, was once a grain warehouse first established in 1885. Today, the stone archways remain, but now they take you to an upscale dining room with candlelit tables, an exquisite bar originally designed on a cocktail napkin, and a menu featuring exotic wild game and, of course, plenty of elevated alligator dishes.

Owner Maureen Craig and her late husband Hilary brought the concept to Savannah only after opening two other restaurants by the same name on the West Coast. "The word 'soul,' simply put, stands for integrity," Maureen told *South* magazine. "It stands for the impact any of us can make in the world each day for good." The word *alligator* takes on a deeper meaning, representing an individual's outer appearance. The two together, Alligator Soul, challenge one to think about how we treat others and where we want the emphasis to be—on the inside or outside—as an individual and as a society. Maureen's husband passed away in 2007, but she says, "He was a man of honor who loved to cook and loved to serve. The joy he felt in taking care of guests was palpable." Maureen and her team carry on that legacy, and you'll experience the attention to detail and genuine appreciation for your visit from the time you walk through the door until you finish your meal.

For more than 20 years, Alligator Soul has forged relationships with local and regional farmers and food purveyors, developing a

Reservations are highly recommended.

Top left: Inside the Colonial cellars of Alligator Soul is a well-appointed fine dining room. *Above left:* New Orleans–style barbecue shrimp with Louisiana Gulf shrimp sautéed in meunière sauce, served with corn bread, honey butter, and crawfish à la soul spinach. *Top right:* A Wild Game Specialty dish featuring antelope. *Above right:* The alligator boudin fritters with peppadew piri piri and creamy dill sauce, garnished with crispy prosciutto.

seasonal menu as unique as their namesake. With selections such as alligator boudin fritters, alligator tempura (meaning deep fried), and deviled alligator crab, the menu features Cajun and Creole influences with a bevy of farm-to-table, local day-boat fish and grass-fed meat options. The diver scallops are a must-try, pan-seared and served with a roasted red pepper cream sauce. On to the Grillades section of the menu, you'll find wild boar shank, duck, and a veal chop served with sautéed mushrooms, a mustard cream sauce, and a pistachio gremolata. Vegetarian and gluten-free items are aplenty.

The wild game specialty dish aims to expose diners to the ever-widening array of culinary delights from around the world, such as elk, antelope, kangaroo, ostrich, game birds, and red deer, subject to availability.

Eat, drink, and relax your soul.

114 Barnard St.
912-232-7899, alligatorsoul.com

TUBBY'S TANK HOUSE THUNDERBOLT

Seafood and Southern favorites

On the bluff across from the shrimp docks in historic Thunderbolt is Tubby's Tank House, a local first choice for seafood and Southern favorites. With a view of the Wilmington River and gentle ocean breezes making their way to the expansive patio surrounded by Spanish moss–covered oak trees, Tubby's Tank House is one of the most laid-back and relaxing dining experiences you can have in the Savannah area. The location is perfect for those on the way to Tybee Island or anyone looking for an inspired menu from the land and sea.

When you drive up to Tubby's you'll see a large gravel parking area to your right. Choose from multiple areas to dine–inside you'll find booths lining the walls, round tables for large parties, and four-top tables scattered throughout the rustic dining room filled with chandeliers made of oyster shells, warm hardwood flooring, and framed images of regional fish adorning the walls. A welcoming indoor bar provides ample seating, but outside on the patio there's an additional bar with flat-screen TVs and an array of refreshing boat drinks and draft beers. A charming covered front porch with ceiling fans and hanging baskets of colorful flowers is also an inviting space to enjoy lunch, dinner, or brunch. No matter where you choose to sit, each space is thoughtfully designed for your enjoyment.

Known for their crispy fried shrimp and signature fresh catch—the local catch of the day, which you can order grilled, blackened, or fried—Tubby's Tank House also offers a variety of sandwiches, salads, and steaks. The crab stew with Georgia blue crab is a popular choice, as are Tubby's tacos with lightly blackened fish or chicken and a piquant

Top left: Tubby's Tank House is a longtime favorite among the locals. *Above left:* Shrimp three ways: buffaloed, steamed, or fried. Photo courtesy of Live Oak Restaurant Group. *Above center:* The tankout platter with shrimp, scallops, oysters, or fish. Photo courtesy of Live Oak Restaurant Group. *Top right:* Views of the Intracoastal Waterway pair perfectly with cold cocktails. *Above right:* Lighter appetite? Try the crab stew and side salad. Photo courtesy of Live Oak Restaurant Group.

black bean and corn salsa, finished with a bright citrus sour-cream drizzle. For those with larger appetites, in the "Anchors" section of the menu are choices of filet mignon, crab cakes, and fettuccine Alfredo.

Don't miss weekend brunch with specialties such as Ansely's omelet, named after the owner, with spinach and Swiss cheese, topped with butterflied shrimp. A brunch burger with a poached egg and sweet selections such as French toast with maple syrup also stand out.

Live music is offered often on the patio, which fills up quickly during football season and around popular Savannah party times, such as St. Patrick's Day. Head on over to Tubby's and raise a glass to good times.

2909 River Dr., Thunderbolt
912-354-9040, tubbysthunderbolt.com

TWO SMART COOKIES

Handcrafted, iced cutout cookies

There's a popular phrase that "a balanced diet is a cookie in each hand," and one family-owned business in Savannah would agree. Started in 2003 by two friends, homemaker Annette Rock and speech therapist Amanda Cannon, Two Smart Cookies is the destination for custom-made cookies in Savannah. Located in Midtown in a two-story home on White Bluff Road, the bakery is famous for its handcrafted, iced cutout cookies, available in a variety of shapes and sizes, and 15 traditional flavors of cookies made from scratch daily.

To keep up with the demand for business, Two Smart Cookies moved from its original home on Hodgson Memorial Drive to its current location in 2007. In 2013, the original owners sold the business to a pair of longtime customers, both financial advisors, Bill Hannah and Ashley Dando. The new owners agreed that Annette and Amanda had created a business model for success. Ashley told the *Savannah Morning News* the challenge with finding good cookies was twofold. "Either the cookies tasted great but weren't pretty, or looked good and tasted bad," she said. "There was only one place we found that had both."

For more than a decade, Ashley and Bill have carried on that success, employing their family members to operate the day-to-day business. Their cookies have been featured in *Southern Living* and *Country Living* magazines, in *Cooking with Paula Deen*, and on CNN Headline News's "Small Business Success," in addition to local media. The bakery features a "Cookie of the Month," which is always a creative, one-of-a-kind flavor, such as lime coconut or chocolate-chocolate with peppermint cookie. On the menu, you'll find local favorites including white chocolate macadamia nut, peanut butter, chocolate chip with pecans, and sugar cookies. Soft, sweet, and baked

Top left: Two Smart Cookies has been Savannah's cookie of choice for 20 years. *Above left:* Cookie cakes are also available for special occasions. *Top right:* An assortment of daily flavors and iced sugar cookies. *Above right:* Iced cutout cookies shaped like foaming mugs of green beer for St. Patrick's Day. All photos courtesy of Two Smart Cookies.

to perfection, the taste is simply irresistible. Other daily selections such as brownies, lemon squares, and rice crispy treats are also available.

As you walk inside the bakery, the enticing aroma of fresh-baked cookies will greet you, but you'll notice baked goods aren't the only thing for sale. Two Smart Cookies has a lobby full of locally made retail goods from honey, candles, and handmade soaps to popcorn and cheese straws. Ready-made Georgia gift baskets showcase the best of the Peach State and Hostess City.

A wall stencil in the vestibule sums up their motto nicely: "Kindness is free. Sprinkle it everywhere."

6512 White Bluff Rd.
912-353-2253, twosmartcookies.com

Two Smart Cookies has a large parking area in front of the bakery.

SLY'S SLIDERS & FRIES

The mecca of mini

There are a lot of good places you can grab a hamburger in Savannah, but there's only one place that makes them mini: Sly's Sliders & Fries, a corner hamburger joint that opened on Abercorn Street in 2014 with a fun philosophy: take your favorites, make them smaller, and have them all. The Southern comfort fusion menu resonates with people of all ages, from college students to tourists and locals. Expect big flavors on small buns.

Sly's is owned by Scott and Laura Wester. Scott comes from a long line of Savannahians, and Laura moved to Georgia in 2012. Inside, there's a walk-up counter where you place your order, then select your drink at the Coca-Cola dispenser. A large chalkboard sign displays the menu, including 11 award-winning signature sliders, famous hand-cut french fries, and seven slider dogs. Fry toppings from fresh jalapeños to fried eggs are listed, along with the sides: black beans, slaw, or salad. To quench your thirst, the menu also includes a variety of ice-cold craft beer and hard cider. Local artwork for purchase decorates the walls, along with framed comics and a painting of a sly red fox honoring the restaurant's namesake.

The Boardwalk is a bestseller and features a beef patty with ketchup, mustard, American cheese, bacon, and dill pickles. A popular vegetarian option is the Shroomwich with marinated

Here's a fun fact: long before it became a slider shop, Scott's great-grandmother worked in the same location when the property functioned as a dry-cleaning and alterations business many years ago.

Left: The Bullet Club Slider with fried chicken with The Boardwalk and hand-cut fries. *Center:* An ice chest with Savannah Square Pops, another locally owned business, offers dessert. *Right:* On-street parking is available at Sly's.

mushrooms, Swiss herb mayo, and a tangy lemon vinaigrette. The slider dog flavors nod to a range of cultures from Cuban to German and, of course, a Chicago dog aptly named the Windy City and properly dressed with a slice of tomato and pickled sport pepper (a small, pale-green pickled pepper with a tangy, spicy bite).

For dessert, Savannah Square Pops are on hand, offering locally inspired frozen treats in assorted flavors. With two dining rooms indoors, seating is also available outside under the covered yellow awning on the pet-friendly sidewalk.

Sly's Sliders & Fries is a fast-casual, cooked-to-order restaurant founded in Savannah. The owners have big plans to turn the establishment into a franchise. Nationally recognized by the *New York Times*, *Woman's Day*, and *Thrillist* for their outstanding sliders, for those indecisive eaters, Sly's takes the guesswork out of the equation.

Who says you can't have it all?

1710 Abercorn St.
912-239-4219, slysslidersandfries.com

ZUNZI'S + ZUNZIBAR

South African–inspired sandwich shop and beach bar

The Hostess City is full of surprises. An igloo is not something typically associated with the humid, subtropical climate of Savannah, but during the short winter months from November to mid-February, there's one happening restaurant that's creating a snow den of its own.

At Zunzi's, a South African–inspired sandwich shop, and its sister beach bar known as Zunzibar, the large patio is transformed into an après ski-themed igloo bar complete with gas heaters, creating an imaginative and fun experience for all who visit. *Après* is a French word meaning "after," and renting an igloo feels much like visiting with friends at a ski lodge following a day on the slopes at your favorite chalet. Accommodating up to eight, the igloos are decked out with warm white lights and tastefully furnished with comfortable seating. Pillows and checkered blankets welcome you around a table filled with card games. Warm winter drinks such as apple cider, hot chocolate, and mulled wine are served to the tune of live music. It's the perfect unpredictable activity for enjoying with a group of friends or as a cozy date night for two.

For most of the year, Zunzibar is a traditional beach bar serving handcrafted cocktails, frozen drinks, wine, and draft and canned beers. Zunzi's menu features award-winning sandwiches served on 12-inch French bread with Zunzi's sauce (tangy and cream-based), wings, bowls, and bar bites. Known for the Conquistador, once named the best sandwich in the South and one of the top three sandwiches in the nation by Travel Channel host Adam Richman, it includes a heaping portion of peri-peri-marinated chicken, provolone and parmesan cheeses, with Zunzi's sauce and dressing. The Rising Sun gives vegetarians reason to smile: portobello mushrooms, squash, and zucchini are paired with hummus and guacamole. A South African sweet tea is also available,

Left: The award-winning Conquistador sandwich is Zunzi's most popular menu item. Photo courtesy of Zunzi's. *Top center:* Customizable igloos are available for rent during the winter months. Photo courtesy of Zunzi's. *Above center:* In 2023, the first stand-alone Zunzibar location opened on Tybee Island, taking the beach bar concept to the beach. Founder and CEO Chris Smith (center), staff, and community members celebrate at the official ribbon-cutting ceremony. Photo courtesy of Casey Jones Photography. *Top right:* No one does happy hour like Zunzibar. Photo courtesy of Zunzi's. *Above right:* The interior of Zunzi's is Instagram worthy. Find your umbrella! Photo courtesy of Zunzi's.

along with nonalcoholic drinks for those who wish not to imbibe.

Zunzi's has a longtime reputation in Savannah; it first opened in 2005 in a small brick building on York Street as a favorite hole-in-the-wall staple for locals and college students. As the restaurant gained notoriety, you could never visit without seeing a line wrapped around the building. Flash forward to present day, and the restaurant has new ownership under cofounder and CEO Chris Smith, a former Five Guys franchisee. Chris purchased the restaurant in 2014 from its original owners, who are from South Africa and Switzerland, with the intent of franchising in the Southeast and beyond.

236 Drayton St.
912-443-9555

1115 US Hwy. 80, Tybee Island
912-472-4902

1971 Howell Mill Rd., Atlanta
470-698-2351, zunzis.com

Zunzi's is home of "Zunzifest!," a quarterly customer-appreciation event involving free sandwiches for the community, fans, and staff.

MOON RIVER BREWING COMPANY

Pub fare with Southern flair

As the city's first luxury hotel and inn built in 1821, the historic building occupied by Moon River Brewing Company has worn many hats over the years. It's full of rich history and today is one of Savannah's most haunted hot spots. Housed in one of the oldest buildings in the city at the corner of Bay and Whitaker Streets, this favorite pub serves up simple comfort food, eclectic gourmet cuisine, and the finest craft beer, 15 barrels at a time. As a restaurant and brewery, with an additional 5,400-square-foot beer garden, Moon River Brewing Company has been helping patrons say "Cheers" for more than 24 years.

The beer is brewed right on Bay Street, with year-round and seasonal specialty options. Selections on "The Regulars" menu range from Southern-style pale ales and Belgian-style wheat ales to American IPAs and robust porters. The Yoga Pants, described as "the perfect marriage of form and function, fashion and comfort, beauty and beast," offers a sophisticated malt profile and brazen hoppiness. Then there's the full-bodied Captain's Porter, a semisweet dark ale with distinct notes of caramel and chocolate. The menu includes helpful notes to guide your food choices, with suggestions for food pairings such as the chicken sandwich or stuffed mushrooms with the Yoga Pants, and for the

John Pinkerton is the president and founder of the Georgia Craft Brewers Guild, a not-for-profit company established to protect and serve the craft brewers of Georgia through regulatory advocacy and promotion of beer tourism and brewery-business development.

Left: The team at Moon River Brewing Company is undeniably passionate about serving great beer. *Center:* Ms. Karen's chicken and sausage creole is a classic menu item featuring boneless chicken breast sautéed with smoked sausage, peppers, tomatoes, onions, and mushrooms, and served over low country rice. *Right:* Moon River Brewing Company is family friendly, with a pet-friendly beer garden, and offers live music often and happy hour every day. All photos courtesy of Moon River Brewing Company and Amber Cossio.

Captain's Porter, the pork shoulder sandwich. Try the Southern-style fried chicken served with mac and cheese and collards, or the Moon Burger, a six-ounce grass-fed beef patty locally sourced from Hunter Cattle Company. Quesadillas, nachos, and loaded tots are other popular accompaniments to enjoy while sipping on your favorite ale.

The restaurant was formerly home to the first US Post Office in the Hostess City, and during the Civil War the second floor functioned as a hospital for soldiers. Over the years, the building has been a lumber and coal warehouse, office supply store, and large printing press. In 1999 proprietor and Brewmaster Emeritus John Pinkerton and his business partner restaurateur Gene Beeco opened Moon River Brewing Company, making a name for themselves and the business in Georgia's craft beer scene. Moon River Brewing Company once won first place in the Classic Irish-Style Dry Stout category at the international World Beer Cup with a beer called the Bomb, developed with a tight, clean roastiness, along with a base malt and UK Target hops meant to "sting just a little bit."

As they say, hot or cold, rain or shine, at the Moon River Brewing Company, the forecast always calls for 100 percent beer drinking weather.

21 W Bay St.
912-447-0943, moonriverbrewing.com

STRANGE BIRD

Chargrilled meats and delectables

When you think of a strange bird, you may envision someone who is not like other people, who marches to the beat of their own drum, and who opposes being fenced in and labeled to fit a certain mold. And that's exactly what the team behind Strange Bird, a neighborhood restaurant serving casual plates with a Mexican flair, would want you to think about the intention behind their menu and concept. "We set ourselves up to be fluid," chef-owner Brandon Carter told Connect Savannah. "The vast majority of dishes will touch the Mexican border in some way, but that doesn't mean that they have to."

The food truck turned brick-and-mortar establishment debuted in the Victorian District at the intersection of Barnard and Henry Streets in a vintage 1930s Streamliner dining car in July of 2023. Offering flavorful lunch and dinner dishes from its in-house smoker in the form of shareables, smokehouse tacos, burritos, tortas, and elevated sides, Strange Bird also has a beverage menu with something for everyone, including creative nonalcoholic cocktails, unique wines, and a rotating list of agua frescas.

Those unfamiliar with the lingo will find the list of "Some Things to Know" at the center of the menu helpful as a key to the restaurant's jargon. For example, "Strange Sauce" is a tomato-based aioli with a blend of 13 spices, and cochinita pibil is a Yucatan-style barbecued pork found in the smokehouse tacos and burritos. The tortas, or Mexican sandwiches, are served patty-melt style on soft, buttery, Parker House–style griddled bread. As for side dishes, the Strange Bird take on refried beans, a classic Mexican side dish, are refried butter beans—what Brandon calls an "OG dish" that has evolved over several years.

The Streamliner diner is owned by the Savannah College of Art and Design (SCAD), and prior to the pandemic, Sandfly Bar-B-Q (page

Top left: The restored vintage Streamliner was purchased by SCAD in 1990 and transported to its current location. Between its original mahogany booths and fixed stools at the marble bar, Strange Bird seats 32 inside. Outdoor seating is also available. *Above left:* Cochinita pibil tacos with oregano, orange, and soy. *Top right:* Queso fundido with pico de gallo, pumpkin seeds, chiles toreados, totopos. You can also add chorizo. *Above right:* Co-chefs de cuisine Felipe Vera and Daniel Aranza. All photos courtesy of SV Images.

30) had occupied the location for five years. Luckily for Strange Bird, the smokehouse with smoker remains behind the building, and they use it to produce all of the meats for their sandwiches, tacos, and burritos.

Strange Bird is helmed by co-chefs de cuisine Daniel "Nilo" Aranza and Felipe Vera, two longtime FARM Hospitality Group culinary team members who bring a lighthearted and playful approach to the menu. Strange Bird is part of the same group that brought Savannah Common Thread and the Wildflower Cafe to Telfair Square. Expect refined street food, locally sourced and in season, made by hand and from scratch with big flavor.

1220 Barnard St.
912-250-9500, strangebirdsavannah.com

On weekdays when Strange Bird is closed, plans are in place to showcase chef residencies and pop-ups featuring out-of-town guest chefs and unique styles of cuisine uncommon in Savannah.

COLLINS QUARTER

Melbourne-inspired coffee café

In 2014, Savannah's food scene grew by leaps and bounds, and one of the restaurants it welcomed offered something refreshingly different: an upscale Aussie-European–style café and coffeehouse known for brunch, which quickly became a part of downtown life. Anchored at the corner of Bull and Oglethorpe, Collins Quarter is the innovation of Australian-born owner Anthony Debreceny, who originally came to the US as a Japanese translator for those seeking to purchase sportfishing yachts. He and his wife had not planned on staying in Savannah long term, but destiny had other plans.

"I'm a guy who admittedly had no idea of the restaurant industry before opening Collins Quarter," he told *Savannah Magazine*. "I like coffee and I like good food. I've never been a chef and I've never worked as a server—my whole experience is as a customer. That's why I push everyone on my team to think like a customer." This philosophy has been hugely successful for Anthony—since opening his flagship restaurant, four other concepts have come to fruition under the Southern Cross Hospitality restaurant group umbrella. In 2019, Collins Quarter opened a second location at Savannah's iconic Forsyth Park with a different menu than the first location, plus a coffee and pastry takeaway window. He also owns the Fitzroy, an Australian pub with panache; the Deck, a chic beach bar on Tybee Island; and his latest, Ukiyo, an urban Japanese ramen bar.

When Collins Quarter first opened, they focused on standard yet innovative breakfast foods and specialty coffee, serving breakfast, lunch, and brunch. Later, they expanded services to include dinner. Bananas Foster French toast, made with brioche bread, candied pecans, and mascarpone, is a brunch favorite. The Israeli-style

Left: Quinoa chicken salad is made with grilled chicken thigh, smashed avocado, and a cilantro cream dressing. Photo courtesy of Collins Quarter. *Center:* Owner Anthony Debreceny inside the Fitzroy. Photo courtesy of Jeremiah Hull for *Savannah Magazine*. *Right:* The Avo Smash is vegan and gluten-free, with three-seeded toast, heirloom tomato, goat feta, beet hummus, avocado, and poached egg. Photo courtesy of Collins Quarter.

shakshouka, a gluten-free dish featuring stone-ground grits, poached eggs, and merguez sausage (a spicy, earthy North African lamb sausage) is also among the more popular dishes. Expect international influences and an eclectic twist on familiar ingredients. In addition to the fresh, healthy food, an extensive wine list, espresso, signature coffees, and craft cocktails are sure to quench your thirst.

The atmosphere has been described as "West Village NYC meets Melbourne, Australia, with a dash of Southern hospitality." With exposed brick walls, modern lighting, and interiors to impress, Collins Quarter is the place to visit for couples and families alike seeking an Aussie brekkie at its best or a down-under breakfast down south.

151 Bull St.
912-777-4147
downtown.thecollinsquarter.com

621 Drayton St.
912-298-6532
forsythpark.thecollinsquarter.com

Southern Living recognized Collins Quarter as one of the "Best Restaurants in Savannah" in 2023.

CHIRIYA'S THAI CUISINE

Thai with a Hawaiian influence

Approximately five miles from downtown Savannah on East Victory Drive, you'll find Chiriya's Thai Cuisine, a charming red-and-white restaurant that packs a big flavor punch. Chiriya Keawcharoen-Moore, a native of Thailand, immigrated to the US in 1976. She attended culinary school in Oahu and met her husband, John, while living in Hawaii. Twenty years later, she and her family moved to Savannah, where she opened her first restaurant showcasing a menu of Thai-Hawaiian fusion and homemade desserts, such as her famous cheesecake. Her love of Hawaiian food and her Thai culture are a match made in heaven on the plate.

For Chiriya's first six years in business, her restaurant was located on the south side of Savannah in Chatham Plaza. That location closed in 2012, but six months later, she and her son and business partner Justin opened a new location in Thunderbolt, where they've been serving elegant Thai cuisine since. Many of Chiriya's family members are employed at the restaurant—Chiriya's sister Miss Bee and niece Pupa can be found prepping the kitchen and creating the crispy, deep-fried spring rolls served with a sweet-and-sour dipping sauce. Chiriya's other sister, Vasannan, and niece Narisa (also known as Jum) are waitresses.

The restaurant is open for lunch and dinner, and the menu includes a variety of appetizers, soups, and salads. A category for Thai noodles features Chiriya's Special Noodles, her signature noodle dish made with broccoli, carrots, and cabbage. The pad se-ew, very popular among the

In 2018 and 2019, Chiriya's Thai Cuisine was voted "Best Thai Restaurant" by the readers of *Connect Savannah*.

Top left: Chiriya's Thai Cuisine at sunset in Thunderbolt. *Above left:* Spring rolls are deep fried with cabbage and carrots, wrapped with clear noodles, and served with a vinaigrette for dipping. *Top right:* Thai Fried Rice with shrimp features jasmine rice, mixed vegetables, eggs, and onions. *Above right:* Behind the restaurant, a quaint garden grows with Thai chili peppers and Thai basil.

Thai locals, is a wide rice noodle dish with stir-fried broccoli, onions, and eggs. There's an array of stir-fried options served over jasmine rice, and six variations of curry made with coconut milk. In Southeast Asia, curry refers to a dish with a sauce or soup base, seasoned with spices. Dishes are available with varying degrees of spiciness, but be prepared: medium may be hotter than you think. Under Hawaiian entrées, you'll find a kalua pig and cabbage dish with smoked pork, slow roasted in banana leaves and stir-fried with cabbage, onion, and Hawaiian sea salt. When your meal is delivered to the table, the server will ask if you'd like chopsticks.

The ambiance is inviting with deep red and orange walls, black ceiling tiles, and coordinating red linens. During service, Chiriya circulates around the two-dining-room space and bar, mingling with guests. A small garden brimming with Thai basil and Thai chili peppers grows out back with ample parking available on-site.

3017 E Victory Dr.
912-691-2080, chiriyasthaicuisine.com

SISTERS OF THE NEW SOUTH

Real Southern cooking

For those in search of the best soul food in Savannah, look no further than Sisters of the New South. Founded by husband-and-wife team Kenneth and Vicky Brown in 2009, Sisters has been synonymous with fried chicken, tender oxtails, and smothered turkey wings since its inception. The Browns are originally from Savannah and have been together since high school. "Everything about us is local," Kenneth says.

The restaurant was named in honor of Vicky and her sisters—Esterline, Janice, Rosa, Betty, Ann, Adele, and Dorothy—many of whom were involved with the concept, and the recipes have been handed down for generations. When they got started, Kenneth's mother-in-law, Mrs. Johnnie Mae Bing, and his mom, Mrs. Scealy Mae Hooker, and his dad gave the couple some recipes.

"We like to say we serve food that built America. Food that you grew up on," says Kenneth. If you grew up in the South, you'll know exactly the kind of timeless food Kenneth is talking about—sweet corn bread, creamy mac and cheese, and meats such as smothered pork chops and juicy hamburger steak. It's the old-school meat and three that never goes out of style. Few places offer a lunchtime special that is more delicious and affordable. "People take for granted in the

In 2023, Sisters of the New South was featured on Food Network's *Diners, Drive-Ins and Dives* with Guy Fieri. Guy told Kenneth that the food was so good, he'd see him next week, to which Kenneth replied, "We'll see you tomorrow." That catchphrase is now on the back of employee T-shirts.

Top left: Three-layer red velvet cake with cream cheese frosting and pecans. Photo courtesy of Sisters of the New South. *Above left:* Fried chicken, collard greens, mashed potatoes, and Savannah red rice is a classic meat and three. Photo courtesy of Sisters of the New South. *Center:* Kenneth Brown, co-owner, who describes himself as, "my wife Vicky's maintenance guy." *Right:* Sisters of the New South is located on busy Skidaway Road with indoor and outdoor seating and ample parking.

South that everybody can make fried chicken and collard greens, but when people come, they realize, no, this ain't something everybody can make," says Kenneth.

Sisters has the solution to that conundrum in their own line of seasonings, each one meticulously created with a special blend, so that anyone can experience what it's like to cook like Grandma with every bit as much love. "One of the biggest compliments we get is when people say, 'This reminds me of my grandmother's cooking or my mom's cooking,'" says Kenneth. "They see the food, and then when they taste the food, they have those memories."

Among the must-try vegetables are the meatless Savannah red rice, collard greens, and candied yams. "We learned that you don't want to put meat in your vegetables, because some people don't eat pork; some people are vegetarian, some are vegan," says Kenneth. "And this was back in 2009. The movement wasn't as strong as it is today, but now, a lot of people appreciate that."

Ironically, there's a national fried chicken fast food chain located directly across the street from Sisters, but on Sundays, Kenneth says no one would even know it was there.

2605 Skidaway Rd.
912-335-2761, sisters4me.com

VIC'S ON THE RIVER

Elegant waterfront dining

Vic's on the River may be one of Savannah's most elegant waterfront dining destinations. Situated in a five-story 19th-century historic brick warehouse on River Street, the restaurant was voted one of the "50 Best Restaurants in America for a Date" by OpenTable. They serve classic Southern seafood with an extensive wine list, and you can dine here for brunch, lunch, or dinner. As you enjoy your meal, be prepared to take in amazing views of the gargantuan cargo ships on the Savannah River while enjoying elevated service to the tune of live piano music nightly.

The lunch menu features a few more sandwiches than the dinner menu, such as the Cheerwine short rib sandwich with a cherry glaze, served on a brioche bun with horseradish cream and arugula. Another crowd-pleaser is the fried green tomato BLT, served with goat cheese and sun-dried tomato pesto on toasted sourdough. Try them with a side of Old Bay french fries or, for a real Southern treat, smoked cheddar-cheese grits. For dinner, popular selections include Chef Kerry's she-crab soup, a creamy Lowcountry favorite. Entrées not to be missed include the jumbo lump crab cakes, Vic's fried chicken, and the Southern BBQ meatloaf served with crispy fried onion rings.

The restaurant bears the name of the late Dr. Irving Victor, who was a well-known and beloved urologist for 41 years. Born and raised in Savannah, Dr. Irving became a physician at the age of 22. He founded emergency medical services in Chatham County and served as the chief of staff at all three Savannah hospitals. He loved cooking and cookbooks, with a collection in the thousands. Later in life, as fate would have it, Dr. Irving went into the restaurant business with two of his neighbors. Together they owned two other

Left: Soft shell crab sandwich and sweet potato fries with a side of Old Bay aioli. *Center:* Vic's on the River has been a Savannah staple for nearly 20 years. Enter through the Vic's Coffee Bar on River Street or the main entrance on East Bay St. *Top right:* Swordfish and Georgia shrimp on a bed of lemon herb risotto, haricot verts, and a puttanesca relish of tomatoes and olives. *Above right:* Prime rib over mashed potatoes with haricot verts. All photos courtesy of Vic's on the River.

restaurants before Vic's on the River opened in January of 2006, becoming a first choice for locals and tourists. Dr. Irving passed away at 97 years old in 2020, leaving behind an indelible mark on the community and a rich legacy.

Black tablecloths, sophisticated furnishings, and consistently delicious cuisine await you at Vic's on the River. Don't leave without getting a breath of fresh air on the ironclad balconies off the main dining room. Here's a tip: the pianist takes requests.

Vic's on the River encourages reservations for those dining inside, but the comfortable outdoor deck is first come, first served. It is seasonal and seated if weather permits. There is no valet or private parking offered, and resort casual attire is recommended.

26 E Bay St.
912-721-1000, vicsontheriver.com

An elevator inside Vic's on the River leads to Vic's Coffee Bar on the first floor, a charming place to grab a cup of joe or a cocktail.

COMMON RESTAURANT

Innovative and wine-forward

"What's in a name?" The famous William Shakespeare line from *Romeo and Juliet* implies that the naming of things is irrelevant. In the case of Common Restaurant, a Savannah gastropub, the culinary and cocktail program is anything but common. It's the kind of place you dine and remember because the experience opens your mind and palate, exposing you to new flavors or flavor combinations you never would have considered. Take the classic Bloody Mary, for example. Common offers a green version instead of red, made with tomatillos versus tomatoes. Mind blown.

Located in the heart of downtown Savannah, smack dab in the hustle and bustle of East Broughton Street, the restaurant occupies a 140-year-old national historic building. You can't miss the bright blue umbrellas anchoring the outdoor sidewalk seating area. Upon stepping inside, the modern lighting and distressed wooden tables capture your attention, as does the expansive bar with a backdrop of metallic tiles and large LED letter lights spelling out B. C-O-M-M-O-N (for Broughton Common). The open-concept dining area features one of the last remaining mezzanines on Broughton Street, a unique intermediate floor installed between the main floor and ceiling, which provides additional dining space with turquoise, tufted seating and a spectacular bird's-eye view of the craft cocktail bar and first floor.

Common Restaurant is the sister restaurant to the Ordinary Pub, a relaxed underground haunt serving bar food and weekend brunch, located just a few doors down, also on Broughton Street.

Left: The Kick'n Pickle (green) house Bloody Mary is made with pickle juice, tomatillos, hot sauce, and vodka. *Center:* A bird's-eye view of the restaurant taken from the mezzanine. Common is open for dinner and weekend brunch. *Right:* The chicken and biscuit plate is a popular weekend brunch item with fried chicken, a sunny-side-up egg, maple butter, and bourbon syrup.

The ever-changing menu, created by Corporate Executive Chef Justin Grizzard and Executive Chef Kenny Tobin, features regionally sourced, fresh produce and meats and cheeses from local purveyors. From the scratch kitchen comes elevated Southern cuisine such as lobster mac and cheese with oyster mushrooms and bacon, or the short rib hot plate featuring braised short ribs with a coffee whiskey glaze, served with corn bread and red wine jam. Don't miss the raw bar selections–enjoy local oysters on the half shell, raw, prepared, or cold smoked.

With elevated cocktails and a wine-forward approach, Common Restaurant offers an award-winning wine list with more than 550 diverse bottles stored in two on-premise cellars. They earned the *Wine Spectator* "Best of Award of Excellence" in 2022 and 2023, which recognizes wine lists that display excellent breadth across multiple wine-growing regions and/or significant vertical depth of top producers, along with superior presentation. Award recipients are considered destinations for serious wine lovers, showing a deep commitment to wine, both in the cellar and through their service team.

118 E Broughton St.
912-777-3742, commonrestaurant.com

Cotton & Rye

RESTAURANTS A-Z

Alligator Soul
114 Barnard St.

Ardsley Station
102 E Victory Dr.

Auspicious Baking Co.
7360 Skidaway Rd.

Baker's Pride
840 E DeRenne Ave.

Baobab Lounge
400 W River St.

Barnes Restaurant
5320 Waters Ave.

Belford's Savannah Seafood and Steaks
315 W Saint Julian St.

Bella Napoli Italian Bistro
18 E State St.

Bella's Italian Cafe
4420 Habersham St.

Big Bon Bodega
2011 Bull St.

Brochu's Family Tradition
2400 Bull St., Ste. 8

Bull Street Taco
1608 Bull St.

Byrd's Famous Cookies
6700 Waters Ave.
213 W Julian St.
423 E River St.
9 Mill Creek Cir. A-2, Pooler

Carey Hilliard's Restaurant
3316 Skidaway Rd.

Charles J. Russo's Seafood
201 E 40th St.
246 Red Cedar St., Bluffton, SC

Chiriya's Thai Cuisine
3017 E Victory Dr.

Circa 1875
48 Whitaker St.

Clary's Cafe
404 Abercorn St.

Cohen's Retreat
5715 Skidaway Rd.

Collins Quarter
151 Bull St.
621 Drayton St.

Common Restaurant
118 E Broughton St.

Common Thread
122 E 37th St.

Cotton & Rye
1801 Habersham St.

Crystal Beer Parlor
301 W Jones St.

Desposito's Seafood
3501 Macceo Dr.

Dottie's Market
207 W Broughton St.

Driftaway Café
7400 Skidaway Rd.

Eastern Wharf
1 Altamaha St.

Elizabeth on 37th
105 E 37th St.

Erica Davis Lowcountry
3209 E Victory Dr.

Finches Sandwiches & Sundries
2600 Mechanics Ave.,
Thunderbolt

Friendship Coffee Company
205 Johnny Mercer Blvd., Ste. 1

Georgia Queen
9 E River St.

Glo's Coffee Corner
1040 King George Blvd., #60

Green Truck Neighborhood Pub
2430 Habersham St.

HUSK Savannah
12 W Oglethorpe Ave.

Jazz'd Tapas Bar
52 Barnard St.

Kayak Kafé
1 E Broughton St.
5002 Paulsen St. (@ 66th)

Leopold's Ice Cream
212 E Broughton St.
Savannah/Hilton Head
International Airport:
400 Airways Ave.

Love's Seafood & Steaks
6817 Chief of Love Rd.

Lulu's Chocolate Bar
42 Martin Luther King Jr. Blvd.
4700 Hwy. 80, Ste. E

McDonough's Restaurant & Lounge
21 E McDonough St.

Molly McGuire's
216 Johnny Mercer Blvd., #1

Moon River Brewing Company
21 W Bay St.

Mrs. Wilkes' Dining Room
107 W Jones St.

Ogeechee Meat Market
6021 Ogeechee Rd.

Paula Deen's The Lady & Sons
102 W Congress St.

Plant Riverside District
400 W River St.

Poe's Tavern
7 Martin Luther King Jr. Blvd.

Rachael's Restaurant & Bar
1190 King George Blvd.

Rancho Alegre Cuban Restaurant
402 Martin Luther King Jr. Blvd.

Rhett
412 Williamson St.

River Street Sweets®
13 E River St.
4515 Habersham St., Ste. 201
32 E Broughton St.

Sandfly Bar-B-Q
8413 Ferguson Ave.

Savannah Coffee Roasters
215 W Liberty St.

Savannah Seafood Shack
116 E Broughton St.

Shuk Mediterranean
1313 Habersham St.

Sisters of the New South
2605 Skidaway Rd.

Six Pence Pub
245 Bull St.

Sly's Sliders & Fries
1710 Abercorn St.

Spanky's Pizza Galley & Saloon
317 E River St.
308 Mall Blvd.
1605 Strand Ave.,Tybee Island
1221 US Hwy. 80 E, Pooler

Starland Café
11 E 41st St.

Starland Yard
2411 Desoto Ave.

Strange Bird
1220 Barnard St.

Sweet Spice Restaurant
5515 Waters Ave.
1024 W US Hwy. 80, Pooler

Tequila's Town Mexican Restaurant
109 Whitaker St.
7360 Skidaway Rd.
13475 Atlantic Blvd., Ste.1, Jacksonville, FL

The Bamboo Room Tiki Bar
116 W Congress St.

The Burger Boat
315-406-0804

The Draft Room at Berwick
5730 Ogeechee Rd., Ste. 110

The Gaslight Group
B. Matthew's Eatery
325 E Bay St.
The 5 Spot
4430 Habersham St.
7360 Skidaway Rd., Unit E-1
3742 Hwy. 17, Richmond Hill
Abe's on Lincoln
17 Lincoln St.

The Grey
109 Martin Luther King Jr. Blvd.

The Little Crown by Pie Society
19 Jefferson St.
1215 E US Hwy. 80, Ste. 200, Pooler

The Olde Pink House Restaurant & Tavern
23 Abercorn St.

The Paris Market Café
36 W Broughton St.

The Pirates' House
20 E Broad St.

The Vault Kitchen + Market
2112 Bull St.

The Wright Square Bistro
21 W York St.

The Wyld Dock Bar
2740 Livingston Ave.

Tubby's Tank House Thunderbolt
2909 River Dr., Thunderbolt

Two Smart Cookies
6512 White Bluff Rd.

Vic's on the River
26 E Bay St.

Vinnie Van GoGo's
317 W Bryan St.

Yia Yia's Kitchen & Marketplace
3113 Habersham St.

Zunzi's + Zunzibar
236 Drayton St.
1115 US Hwy. 80, Tybee Island
1971 Howell Mill Rd., Atlanta

Eggs and ham from Clary's Cafe

Cleary's
CAFE

The Gaslight Group's B. Matthew's Eatery Bacon Mary, Courtesy of Blake Studwell.

APPENDIX

DOWNTOWN

Crystal Beer Parlor, 8
Kayak Kafé, 16
Savannah's Seafood Shack, 10
Mrs. Wilkes' Dining Room, 12
The Grey, 72
The Pirates' House, 22
Bella Napoli Italian Bistro, 112
The Olde Pink House Restaurant & Tavern, 56
Elizabeth on 37th, 74
McDonough's Restaurant & Lounge, 60
Paula Deen's The Lady & Sons, 34
Common Thread, 118
Circa 1875, 98
The Paris Market Café, 104
Moon River Brewing Company, 156
Six Pence Pub, 128
Big Bon Bodega, 26
The Bamboo Room Tiki Bar, 18
HUSK Savannah, 20
Leopold's Ice Cream, 46
Rhett, 138
Lulu's Chocolate Bar, 124
Jazz'd Tapas Bar, 130
Alligator Soul, 146
Savannah Coffee Roasters, 86
Zunzi's + Zunzibar, 154
Baobab Lounge, 36
Plant Riverside District, 38
Clary's Cafe, 52
River Street Sweets®, 68
Common Restaurant, 168
The Gaslight Group, 100
Dottie's Market, 114
Poe's Tavern, 122
The Wright Square Bistro, 126
Rancho Alegre Cuban Restaurant, 134
Shuk Mediterranean, 140
Sly's Sliders & Fries, 152
Collins Quarter, 160
Vic's on the River, 166

CITY MARKET

Belford's Savannah Seafood and Steaks, 62
The Little Crown by Pie Society, 64
Vinnie Van GoGo's, 82

SOUTHSIDE

Ogeechee Meat Market, 14
Carey Hillard's Restaurant, 40
The Draft Room at Berwick, 102
Love's Seafood & Steaks, 4

GEORGETOWN

Rachael's Restaurant & Bar, 132
Glo's Coffee Corner, 84

MIDTOWN

Baker's Pride, 6
Byrd's Famous Cookies, 44
Bella's Italian Cafe, 90
Green Truck Neighborhood Pub, 76
Barnes Restaurant, 42
Ardsley Station, 94
Spanky's Pizza Gallery & Saloon, 70
Two Smart Cookies, 150
Sweet Spice Restaurant, 80